Soar...
If You Dare ™

& Use Your
SECRET POWERS
FOR SUCCESS
To Make Your Dreams Come True!

James R. Ball

Published by Humdinger™ Books

We don't print it unless it's a Humdinger.

Soar...
If You Dare™

& Use Your
SECRET POWERS
FOR SUCCESS
To Make Your Dreams Come True!

Soar: to fly, often at great height; to rise or increase dramatically in position or value; to ascend to a higher or more exalted level; to rise to majestic stature.

Humdinger™ Books may be purchased in quantity for educational,
business, promotional, and similar use.

Printed in the United States of America

First Edition

Humdinger™ Books
ISBN: 0-9633184-9-7

Published in the United States by:
Humdinger™ Books
A Division of
The Humdinger™ Corporation
P.O. Box 3736
Reston, Virginia 22090-1736

Library of Congress Cataloging-in-Publication Data
Ball, James R.
Soar . . . If You Dare: Secret Powers For Success
Library of Congress Catalog Card Number: 92-71838

For information, please write:
Humdinger™ Books
P.O. Box 3736
Reston, VA 22090-1736

Notice: *Soar . . . If You Dare* and
Humdinger are trademarks of
The Humdinger Corporation.

For Dolly, Jennifer, and Stephanie,
and for
Mom, Dad, and Bud

Special Acknowledgements and Thanks

There are numerous sources for the many quotations and anecdotes in this work and authors have been credited where possible. I greatly appreciate the work of these authors and their publishers.

I also want to thank Vicki Shannon, business copy chief at *The Washington Post,* for her superb editorial assistance; Paul Gormont of Apertures, Inc., for his creativity in design and layout; Craig Cartwright for his brilliant illustrations; Steve and Ann Hunter at AAH Graphics for their assistance in packaging this entire work; Mel Baughman and Lisa Champagne at Lanman Progressive for their tremendous help with the cover; and George Gingerelli of Delta Research Corporation, and Joe Andahazy and Debbi Parrish of Listen2Books for their collective contribution to the title of this work.

Most importantly, I want to thank Jennifer Kuchta, the person who prodded me to write *Soar . . . If You Dare*. This work never would have been possible without Jennifer's many contributions—her input was invaluable.

DO YOU know why grownups are always asking little kids what they want to be when they grow up?

It's 'cause they're looking for ideas.

—**Paula Poundstone**

Table of Contents

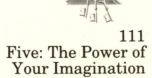

Dear Reader:

WHEN I was six years old and on vacation with my family, I would lie awake, long after I was supposed to have gone to sleep, and imagine myself finding a magic bottle on the beach. I envisioned uncorking the bottle and summoning a powerful genie to grant my wishes and provide me more riches than a thousand carts could haul away.

Years have passed, but beneath my adult facade, there is a kid inside who still believes in genies and *Genie Power*.

I know now that Genie Power is a *little* different than I imagined it as a kid, but it exists just the same. I also have learned that I'm not the only one with

Genie Power. Everyone has it. And I really do mean everyone!

> *You see children know such a lot now, they soon don't believe in fairies, and every time a child says, 'I don't believe in fairies,' there is a fairy somewhere that falls down dead.*
> —from *Peter Pan*
> by James Matthew Barrie

    I've written this book because so many people have lost the kid in themselves, stopped imagining, and no longer see themselves attaining their wildest dreams. This is a problem. A big one.

    I've taught sessions at universities and found that many students have an apathetic view of life; in truth, a good number of them do not expect to make much of themselves. Similarly, I know adults, some of them highly educated, who have given up on their ambitions or who have a very low sense of what they can accomplish. A psychologist I know who specializes in helping people with low self-esteem is never at a loss for clients. Worse, I know a *child* psychologist who believes the biggest problem kids face today is a low sense of self-worth. That individuals aren't striving for greatness concerns me, but what really worries me is that *most of them haven't even considered that greatness is one of their options*—they no longer *dream* of the possibilities.

An uninspired mind is a handicap we all can do something about. Millions of people are just drifting along when so much more is possible. And I don't mean a little bit more, I mean a lot more—a whole lot more. In the world we live in, we all can be stretching for the stars and reaching them, but some individuals are so busy just spending their lives that they have forgotten about dreaming, and Genie Power, and all the other powers at their disposal—the Secret Powers for Success, as I call them.

> *To dream anything that you want to dream. That is the beauty of the human mind. To do anything that you want to do. That is the strength of the human will. To trust yourself to test your limits. That is the courage to succeed.*
>
> —Bernard Edmonds

Someone once said that the obscure we will see right away, but the obvious takes a little longer. As Oliver Wendell Holmes wrote: *We need education on the obvious more than investigation of the obscure.* That is the way it often is for these secret powers— they are *so* obvious we overlook them.

In this book, I have brought together the keys that will help you re-learn how to dream—and how to make your dreams your realities. This book is not about searching for your weaknesses and being critical of them; rather, it is about finding your strengths and building on them. You have powers you never dreamed you had—you really do—and these powers are presented as tools through a few easy-to-understand and easy-to-remember concepts that fit together like the pieces of a puzzle. Through metaphors, anecdotes, pictures, examples, and quotes, these powers and concepts can become real and easily applied to your life today. In every instance, I've tried to keep it simple.

I hope I have written a book that you not only *can* use, but *will* use to discover the powers within you. My wish is to rekindle the fire in you and to make you think about the most important part of your life, you. You are the greatest miracle in your life, and you were born for greatness. I truly believe that.

I hope that my genie will grant my wish that you will enjoy *Soar . . . If You Dare* and that it will change your life in some positive way.

Dare to dream. And please let me know how it's going—I'd be delighted to hear from you.

Jim Ball
Humdinger™ Books
P. O. Box 3736
Reston, VA 22090-1736

One

You have secret powers you never
dreamed of. You really do. And you can
use these powers to achieve whatever you
want in life. You really can.

You Possess Secret Powers

THINK ABOUT THIS. When was the last time some-one said to you: "Hey, you. Why don't you take some time to figure out what you want out of life and how you can get it?" Or who ever told you: "Guess what? You can be whatever you want to be—you really can. You can be the one to save the rain forests, if that's what you want. You can be the one to cure cancer. You can paint the most famous painting ever. You really can do any of these things if you want to. Did you know that?"

Well, that's exactly what I'm saying to you now. *You really can.*

Compared to what we ought to be, we are only half awake, famed psychologist and philosopher William James of Harvard University wrote years ago. *We are making use of only a small part of our physical and mental resources. Stating the thing broadly, the human individual thus lives far within his limits. He possesses powers of various sorts which he habitually fails to use.*

If what James wrote is true, and I believe it is, that leads us to the questions of why this is so, and what can we do about it. Why on earth would we use only a small part of our minds? What good reasons would there be for us to live far within our limits? What possible powers could we have that we are not using?

That's what this book is all about. Most people are so busy just getting through today that they never take the time to think about those questions, ponder how to get the most out of what they have to work with, or figure out what to spend their time on in the first place.

This book lets you ask and answer those questions. It is about the powers we all have that we don't use to our full advantage. It's about developing skills and techniques that will let us use more of the mental capacities we each have. And it's about getting over our limitations and pressing ourselves beyond our limits as we now know them.

There are powers inside of you, which, if you could discover and use, would make of you everything you ever dreamed or imagined you could become.

—Orison Swett Marden

Here, in this book, you will find the powers you can use to get what you want in life. Like laser beams burning through steel, these powers can be yours, to bring you to your destination and to burn through the obstacles you may encounter on your paths to success. These powers are the real thing. They really work. But you have to take time to put them into practice.

In Sum . . .

♦ We use only a small part of our mental resources.

♦ We live far within our limits.

♦ We possess *powers* we habitually fail to call upon; they are the real thing, they really work—but it takes practicing to use them.

How To Approach This Book

Read with a pencil in hand for underlining and making notes. As you read, *slow down* and ponder each of the main points being made, and in your pondering, think about how the examples and the principles apply to *you* and how you can apply the principles in *your* life.

At the conclusion of your reading, flip through the pages once again and summarize all your underlining and notes. Don't rewrite everything you underlined or noted—summarize. After you have done this for each chapter, what you will then be left with are your notes, and what is in your notes is what you will have a chance to apply in life.

Most people have the greatest intentions of applying the important principles they read in books, yet in reality we know that this simply doesn't happen.

Your summarized notes are critical because within a few weeks' time, everything else you have read in this book, except for any thoughts that hit you like a revolutionary thunderbolt, will just settle back onto the pages and soon be forgotten. Only the thoughts in your notes have a chance for survival.

In Sum . . .

◆ Your *summary* notes are critical—only those thoughts have a chance for survival.

By The Book

Think of your reading here as a journey we are going on to learn what you want in life and to discover what secret powers you have which you can use to fulfill your dreams. Through quotes selected because of their pertinence and placed at important milestones along our path, in over two hundred instances we are going to hear what wise men and women have said about the topics we will cover.

What you have in your hands is a two-fold summary—it's a summary of my experiences, but it's also a summary of important points stressed by numerous other individuals in their works and teachings over the years, all of whom have influenced my thinking. While such a summary is useful and time-saving, more importantly, what you have in your hands is an organized method for studying the vast body of self-help knowledge so that you may actually put it to practical use in your everyday life. Knowledge without a method for applying it is of little value. Because of this, like tons and tons of coal compressed to make a single diamond, each chapter has been compressed into a simple, illustrated metaphor and these have been included at the front of the chapters as reminders of the basic principles covered which you can apply in *your* life.

> *Almost all men are intelligent. It is method*
> *that they lack.*
> —Frederick W. Nichol

We begin our journey by taking an up-front look at *The Anacondas in Life*, the limitations we allow to be placed on ourselves. The discussion of Anacondas comes first because if you don't know what the limitations and obstacles are, it's nearly impossible to conquer them and unleash your powers.

After you discover what to avoid, you are introduced to the enigma of BELIEF. Over and over, it has been written that belief is a requirement for achieving what we want. The big problem for many individuals is not with the theory, but with *getting to the point of believing what you don't yet believe.* There is a little magic involved here, an invisible fence you must leap, an inner force that you must draw on that I call *Genie Power.*

Then, after *Genie Power,* one by one, you will learn the other powers that we each have but don't always remember and don't always use to our fullest advantage. These powers aren't unique or totally unknown to you, but they are *secret powers* nonetheless. The problem is that these powers are so downright obvious that we overlook them. They may be only "sort of obvious." They often don't become a part of our consciousness until they are pointed out with logic and clarity. Once that is done, of course, we need to learn how to apply these powers effectively in our daily living.

All of these powers—*Choice, Imagination, Action, Concentration, Habit,* and a power I refer to as the *Ultimate Power*—in addition to *Genie Power*, make up the core of your Secret Powers For Success. There is much, much more to each of these secret powers than appears on the surface. Remember that these are *powers* we are talking about here. Not principles. Not theories. Not laws. Not wishful daydreams. Each of these is a power—a force you can use to get what you want in life.

In Sum . . .

♦ The powers in this book are your Secret Powers For Success—you can use these forces to get what you want in life.

Putting The Powers To Use

Once you have compiled your notes, refer to your thoughts every few days while beginning to develop new habits in applying the techniques you have learned. We lose knowledge that we don't use or refer to periodically, and the drop-off is rather quick, so begin applying these techniques within 24 hours of summarizing your notes. *This is important. Very important.*

A final suggestion I have is that you re-read the whole book every six months or so—at least a breezy read. Every book worth reading is worth reading several times, and I hope you will find that to be the case with *Soar . . . If You Dare.*

You can be the one to save the rain forests. *You* can be the one to write the most beautiful music the world has heard. *You* can be the one to find the cure for cancer. *You really can* be the one.

In Sum . . .

♦ *You* can be the one, you really can.

You are greater than you think you are.
—Norman Vincent Peale

You Possess Secret Powers
What To Do . . .

1. Read the entire book in a few, uninterrupted sittings while making notes and underlining. Make a second pass, this time summarizing your notes.

2. Begin to apply the concept and powers immediately, within 24 hours of completing your note summation. Re-read the whole book periodically.

*Why should
you be content
with so little?
Why shouldn't
you reach out
for something
big? . . .*

—Charles L. Allen

TWO

The greatest obstacles you face in life are the unseen snakes in the road that are ready to strike. To achieve success you must learn how to avoid them or defeat them.

The Anacondas In Life

MOST PEOPLE don't get what they want out of life. Remarkable, isn't it? What's even more incredible is that often it's because of unseen obstacles they don't even know exist.

Achieving success is largely a matter of overcoming opposition, and accomplishing this is impossible unless you know what the opposition is and have some idea how to deal with it.

As Orison Swett Marden, the founder of *Success* magazine, put it years ago: *Success is not measured by what a man accomplishes, but by the opposition he has encountered . . .*

The greatest opposition to success is not the obstacles we see, the ones we already have identified. Rather, it is an unseen nest of snakes in the road. To pass, we must first understand the beasts and then learn how to defeat or avoid them. If we don't, we will slip into their pit and they will swallow us whole.

I call these unseen obstacles the Anacondas in life, named after the tropical snake that grows up to 30 feet long and squeezes the life out of its prey before devouring it. The Anacondas I'm talking about live all around us, in our homes, where we work, where we learn, and where we play. These Anacondas are all of the people, thoughts, and circumstances standing by, waiting to strike and snuff out our dreams, sap our energy, and drain our resources. Given a chance, they will crush out life itself.

Anacondas are the individuals who remind us of the risks and who make us question our self-esteem, our self-worth, and our capabilities. Anacondas are the ones who tell us what we can and can't do, and although we don't ask, they're the ones who define what is possible and what is *not* possible with words like: "You're too young," "you're too short," "you don't have enough money," or "you missed your chance." We tend to not even notice phrases like these or we brush them off. But if we hear these phrases repeated often enough from people we love and respect, they'll crush us by reinforcing our fears and misconceptions.

> *If you succeed in life, you must do it in spite of the efforts of others to pull you down. There is nothing in the idea that people are willing to help those who help themselves. People are willing to help a man who can't help himself, but as soon as a man is able to help himself, they join in making his life as uncomfortable as possible.*
>
> —Edgar W. Howe

Anacondas are particularly onerous because they are so difficult to recognize. Some are chameleon-like masters of disguise; others are entirely invisible. Many Anacondas have split personalities—they are Jekyll-and-Hyde types who transform with a change in the wind from loving, caring friends to bone-crushing beasts.

There are a variety of Anacondas: the Anaconda Dream Snatchers; the Anacondas of Limitation Thinking; the Anacondas of Doubt and Despair; the Anacondas of Undeservedness; the Anaconda Time Bandits; and a special Anaconda which I'll name later, which can be the worst of them all. We need to be on the lookout for all of these beasts—for each species has its own unique crushing coils and we need to understand our powers over each of them.

In Sum . . .

♦ Most people don't get what they want out of life because of the unseen nest of snakes in the way.

Dream Snatchers

Dream Snatchers are Anacondas that do just what their name implies—they steal dreams. No more diabolical a spell could be cast upon an individual than to snatch away their dreams, for it wrenches away a chunk of their spirit.

Consider the little girl dreaming of becoming a ballerina only to have her loving mother transform into a Dream Snatcher with this: "But that takes years of practice and lots of money that we don't have, honey." The little girl may never know she was bitten, but her dream was snuffed out just the same.

A boy I grew up with dreamed of becoming a singer. When he sang solo parts in church, it was impossible not to recognize how good he was. In his late teens, the young man had an opportunity to pursue a musical career as one of the singers with a now-famous country band. But here were the problems, as pointed out to the young man by his mother: "You don't have any money, what are you going to do for money? How will you buy costumes? You can't perform in blue jeans, you know. And where are you going to live—we don't know anybody in Nashville, for crying out loud. You know, you'll have to get a driver's license in Tennessee. How are you going to do that?" To make a long, sad story short, the young man is now an unskilled laborer in a manufacturing plant. His main concern these days is whether he'll be laid off. The worst thing is he never sings anymore, and nobody ever gets to hear his joy.

Have you ever observed an excited little boy run up to his father or mother with a crayon picture he had just spent an hour laboring over? All the father or mother has to say is something like, "Oh, how nice dear, but I'm busy," or like, "Not now honey, daddy's watching television." This is dream snatching at its ugliest.

Dream-snatching moments like these don't happen just in childhood, they happen all through life.

> *Caution! The left-brained world wants you to*
> *"get your head out of the clouds, get your feet*
> *on the ground, and be just like us." To*
> *advance and prosper, steadfastly ignore that*
> *advice.*
>
> —Marilyn Grey

A high school teacher I know spent several months planning what he called his *dream* course, a new course he intended to propose to the principal. I watched my friend's dream *almost* get snatched away over a cookie.

At a reception, my friend went up to the principal at the punch bowl and commented that he had been working on a new course. "It's really revolutionary . . ." my friend began, only to have the principal interrupt him with this: "Oh look! Chocolate chip cookies. My favorite."

My friend was so discouraged by this blow that he quietly left the reception and literally was ready not only to stop his work on the course, but to leave that school system! Reactions like this do happen. We humans are very fragile and it is all too easy to forget this.

In a *McCall's* article entitled *9 Things A Mother Never Should Say*, Stanley Turkei writes: *It's not a bad idea to spot-check our own habitual ways of talking to our kids*. Comments like, "Look how well behaved your brother is" chip away at one child's self-esteem by comparing him to his brother. Or, "Stop crying this instant!" can be interpreted as "Shut up, I don't want to deal with you." These and others can become Anaconda-like comments if they are repeated often enough.

Dream Snatchers can be painfully obvious, like the person who says, "Quit living in a dream world." But they aren't always obvious and, ironically, the

Dream Snatchers who can do the most damage are often the people closest to us: our parents, our families, our close friends, and our colleagues. With all the Dream Snatchers at our feet, it's no wonder that so few people choose to dream and go for greatness.

The easy choice is to let the Dream Snatchers have their way, thus settling for less from life.

> *Ridicule is the weapon most feared by enthusiasts of every description.*
> —Sir Walter Scott

The right choice is to refuse the Dream Snatchers entry, to clutch onto your dreams and bring them into reality in spite of the Dream Snatcher's efforts. A great example of doing just this was reported in the Spring 1992 issue of *Possibilities,* Dr. Robert Schuller's publication. Chris Burke, a star on the ABC series *Life Goes On*, became an actor despite his Down's Syndrome because he and his family learned how to deal with the dream-snatching Anacondas around them. Chris's brother attributes Chris's success to the fact that their family "did not put any limitations on Chris" and they "never listened to those people who wanted to put limitations on him." Chris said that when he told his teachers and others about his dreams to become an actor, people said they "didn't think it would happen." Chris overcame these Anacondas by *choosing* to believe in himself. "I always thought my dreams could happen," Chris said. "I believed in my dreams."

> *Why do so many people let their dreams die unlived? The biggest reason, I suppose, is the negative, cynical attitudes of other people.*
> —Og Mandino

Believing in your dreams is not easy, but you already have the force required to combat Dream Snatchers because you can *choose* to believe in your dreams, and you can *choose* to believe in yourself. Along with your power of choice, several techniques can help you win out over the Dream Snatchers.

One of the best ways to deal with Dream Snatchers is to avoid them. I do this whenever possible. You won't find me hanging around negative thinkers (or Impossibility Thinkers, as Dr. Schuller refers to them). Instead, I make a special effort to keep company only with upbeat, positive thinkers who are gracious enough not to trample my visions.

But some Dream Snatchers, like family members or business associates, are not easily avoidable. In these cases, you can take steps either to limit your time with them or to control the conversation and topics of discussion. "I've gotta run," is something I've said to get away from many Anacondas in life.

This works for me, but it may not suit your personality. The point is you must find a way that you are comfortable with to avoid Dream Snatchers and Dream-Snatching conversation or find ways to counterbalance Dream Snatching remarks whenever possible—even if the Dream Snatcher is a close friend or a loved one.

In Sum . . .

♦ With all the Dream Snatchers snatching away our dreams, it's no wonder that we then don't go for greatness.

♦ We each need to learn to deal with the Dream Snatchers in our lives. We must refuse them our dreams.

Anacondas of Limitation Thinking

Aerodynamically, the bumblebee should not be able to fly. But the bumblebee doesn't know it, so it goes on flying anyway.
—Mary Kay Nash

The Anacondas of Limitation Thinking are the snakes in life that establish the boundaries of our beliefs, expectations, and aspirations. They operate like the invisible electric fences buried in the ground that keep dogs in a yard. When dogs stray near the concealed fence, they get a jolt and jerk back. In time, the fence doesn't even have to have a charge to work because once jolted, the dog never forgets—the memory of the jolt remains.

People are the same in this respect. Once they perceive a limitation, they tend to remember it unwaveringly. It is near impossible for us to go beyond a limitation once it gets into our minds. The story of Cliff Young relates how perceptions of limits become the actual limits until something occurs to change them.

Cliff Young was an unknown, 61-year-old Australian from the back country who showed up a few years ago to enter a long-distance race between Sydney and Melbourne, a distance of about 600 kilometers. Cliff explained that his only running experience was chasing stray animals on his farm, and yet here he was competing in a race against world-class runners. People laughed when Cliff Young entered the race, in his coveralls and work boots no less, but they stopped laughing when he won—beating the person who came in second by a day and a half!

Cliff Young had the advantage of *not* having preconceived mental limitations. The other runners were programmed into thinking that the way to run this race was to run for eighteen hours and rest for six hours. They were victims of Limitation Thinking. Cliff had never run such a race before, so he had no knowledge of the erroneous "ground rules." He just started and ran straight through until he finished.

The following year Cliff's record was broken by a number of runners, but only because Cliff Young had removed the mental limitation for them.

It is amazing what ordinary people can do if they set out without preconceived notions.
—Charles F. Kettering

Girls aren't good at math. How many times have you heard that limitation seed or one like it planted in your lifetime? Girls aren't good at math—to say this is a national crime because it simply isn't true. There isn't a shred of evidence that supports the assertion that girls aren't good at math, nor is there a shred of evidence to support the corollary assertion that they *can't* be good at math, and yet this limiting thought is pounded into the heads of young women over and over throughout their lives. The result is that many of them now believe the assertion and are going about fulfilling their beliefs.

A friend of mine relates this story, which illustrates my point. This friend took her daughter to the doctor for her daughter's annual physical. During the exam, the doctor asked the daughter if she was excited about being a sophomore, which, of course, the daughter was. The doctor asked what subjects the daughter would be taking and geometry was mentioned. To this the female doctor said something like: "Geometry. Ugh. I had trouble with geometry, but then I guess all girls do. I read somewhere that there is something different about females in their ability to work with shapes like boxes and triangles, things like that."

Can you believe it? It's a true story. And you just know my friend's daughter did poorly in geometry. Why? Because girls aren't good at math? Absolutely not! It's because many people, some doctors included, aren't good at recognizing or understanding the impact of their limitation programming and broadcasting. The chances of a fifteen-year-old to *not* believe what her family doctor tells her are remote, so it becomes a very difficult job to negate the erroneous programming of this example.

There is no telling how many ways each of us has been entrapped by Anacondas of Limitation Thinking establishing false limits in our minds as real.

> *Scientists have proven that it's impossible to long-jump 30 feet, but I don't listen to that kind of talk. Thoughts like that have a way of sinking into your feet.*
> —Carl Lewis

As Confucius said: *The Master was entirely free from . . . conclusions . . .* You were not brought into life with limitations. Limitations have been cast upon us like a net and we must cast them off. To overcome Limitation Thinking, we must take actions to broaden our choices.

Regina Taylor, a star on the television series *I'll Fly Away*, who has also been successful on Broadway, put it this way: Acting "teaches you about the possibilities that you can become anything . . . that there aren't any limitations. You shouldn't put limitations on yourself."

In Sum . . .

◆ Anacondas of Limitation Thinking limit us in many ways, and we must take actions to broaden our horizons so we don't allow our own thoughts and the ideas of others to be our boundaries in life.

Anacondas Of Doubt And Despair

The Anacondas of Doubt and Despair are specialists; they impose limitations on us by always being on the lookout for what can go wrong or by constantly wringing their hands while chanting about doom and gloom. If you have persons in your life who are always complaining—about the economy, how unfair life is, how bad the educational system is, the rotten traffic, ad infinitum—get them off their negative trains of thought quickly. One way to do this is to simply change topics by popping a positive note into the conversation such as: "Wasn't Sunday an incredibly beautiful day?" Something like, "Excuse me, have you lost weight? You look terrific" is about as easy a conversation changer I know of. Negative thoughts are contagious, but so are positive ones. With practice, changing to positive topics is an easy *habit* for us to acquire.

Anacondas of Doubt often are responsible for an imagination-limitation best known as the fear of failure. The fear of failure is an actual obstacle of the mind that consists of nothing more than creating and playing mental videos of what you *don't* want to happen. Mental imagery can be a very powerful force, but it is a double-edged sword, with the fear of failure as the negative side of the sword at its ugliest.

The fear of failure can literally kill you. I know of this happening in a business situation where a man committed suicide because he was so afraid of impending financial disaster.

Worry affects the circulation, the heart, the glands, the whole nervous system, and profoundly affects the health. I have never known a man who died from overwork, but many who died from doubt.
— Charles W. Mayo

Anacondas of Doubt and Despair must be dealt with because they can lead you to ruin. The best way to deal with Anacondas of Doubt is to avoid them completely or as much as possible. Absent this, the only solution is to cast their images of doubt from your mind and replace them with positive images of success. Similarly, the grumblings of a doomsayer Anaconda of Despair must be counteracted with positive, reinforcing self-talk.

In Sum . . .

♦ Anacondas of Doubt and Despair limit our expectations of what is possible and invoke our fear of failure.

♦ We must eliminate doubt, despair and other limitations from our minds and replace them with positive beliefs, positive expectancy, and positive self-talk.

Anacondas Of Undeservedness

"People get what they deserve."

How many times have you heard that one? People get what they deserve in life. While this sometimes is in reference to cause and effect—that is, rewards or punishments for our actions—this statement also subtly suggests that someone sat in judgment when each of us was born and decided what each of us deserved. We all know this proposition is ludicrous and yet, in reality, most individuals believe it to some degree. Although most individuals may not think about it consciously, deep inside their subconscious minds, they believe they will get what they "deserve," and some notion of what that is already exists.

Many individuals have not previously considered the concept of Deservedness, which is this: *We cannot achieve more in life than what we believe in our heart of hearts we deserve to have.* In other words, we feel either *Deserved* or *Undeserved* of everything in life. If you think about it, you likely do have a Deservedness Limitation (or an Undeservedness Limitation depending on how you look at it) about various goals you might pursue. This aspect of our imaginations establishes our boundaries of achievement.

Here is something that you may not find very startling: Most people who say they want to be millionaires will never actually achieve this goal. While many individuals may not be serious when they say they want to be millionaires, perhaps there is a reason. Perhaps it is because they don't believe, in their heart of hearts, that they deserve to have that much money or that they will actually be able to get it. A big part of why some individuals won't become millionaires is they honestly can't even imagine themselves acquiring a million dollars in any way other than winning the lottery.

One of the limitations we each face in life is our perceptions of what we deserve to become, based largely on our "station in life": "If my parents weren't millionaires, why should I be one? Am I better than my parents?" It is this kind of deservedness thinking that we need to address and get beyond.

This isn't to say that because of our sense of *deservedness* factors we can't achieve goals beyond those our role models achieved, because we certainly can and thousands of individuals do this all the time. But it does mean that there could be a huge mental obstacle in your roadway, chiseled into the walls of your subconscious mind by the Anacondas you've encountered in your life.

I used the example of a millionaire because money is universally understood. However, the deservedness principle pertains to all kinds of goals, objectives and wants in life. If you don't believe you deserve to be the one to win the gold medal, it is hard to imagine that you will win it. If you don't believe you deserve that promotion, it is hard to imagine why someone else would go out of their way to disagree with you. And if you can't *imagine* achieving your goals, your subconscious mind can't go to work to achieve them. It is this simple: If you don't believe you deserve something, you will have difficulty imagining getting it, and this in turn will limit what you actually achieve.

By the time most of us reached our teens, we already had been programmed with specific senses of internal worth and deservedness. Absent a strong external stimulus or a strong will from within, the sense of deservedness that each of us created in our minds by the time we were teenagers will remain unchanged for life.

The important point is that you can change your sense of deservedness through reprogramming. You deserve the very best in life, and you alone can pick and choose what that is. No one sits in judgment of you and determines what you do and do not deserve to get out of life. Unfortunately, however, there is another reality: You get what *you think* you deserve in life, and there have indeed been a whole host of people who have influenced your deservedness thinking. Henry Ford said: *Whether you think you can or think you can't, you're right.* Whether you think you deserve something or think you don't will affect whether you think you can get it.

The people who have dampened your personal self-worth are the Anacondas of Undeservedness. Almost everyone has been wrapped up in the coils of one or more of these reptiles along the way.

The only effective way to deal with an Anaconda of Undeservedness is to create and hold images of what you truly deserve in life, and that, of course, is whatever you want to have. The answer for dealing with an Anaconda of Undeservedness is to use the power of positive mental images. Mental images will come true.

In Sum . . .

♦ Anacondas of Undeservedness will limit our beliefs as to what we deserve, if we let them.

♦ We must create positive images in our minds of achieving or acquiring what we deserve in life—and *that* is the very best.

Anaconda Time Bandits

Time Bandits are tremendously destructive, yet they are the most tolerated of all the Anacondas. This is perplexing and disturbing when you consider the damage they inflict—they *waste* your time and they *spend* your time. What is time, if not your life? Thus,

Time Bandits are wasting and spending your life, if you let them.

The most squandering of all Time Bandits is mindless, content-free TV shows. The average American watches television about 20 hours each week—that is 12% of a day, but worse than that, it's 18% of the normal waking hours in a day—that's one-fifth of a lifetime! If the average American lives to be 90, then he or she will have spent 18 years in front of the tube! Can this be good? Of even the news, how informed do we have to be? Is it necessary that we watch the morning news, the six o'clock news, the eleven o'clock news, and then read about the same stories in the paper and in magazines on top of that? Do we really have to be *that* informed? Do we really have to know about every killing, every bank or business failure, every skirmish in every country, and every other piece of spicy *bad* news that is occurring in the world?

I don't think so and Thomas Jefferson didn't either. He said: *I do not take a single newspaper, nor read one a month, and I feel myself infinitely the happier for it.*

> *Crime rarely fails to make the headlines. How one wishes there were some way of featuring and dramatizing good living and high thinking.*
> —Robert J. McCracken

The objective is to spend time accomplishing what you want to accomplish in life and wasting time is an Anaconda in the way of your success. A little TV for relaxation and enjoyment is one thing, but watching hours and hours of mindless TV shows is like having a big fat Time Bandit Anaconda on the back of the couch in the family room. Getting ten or eleven hours sleep if you only need eight is like having an Anaconda in your bed. Chatting away about little insignificances on the phone is a big time waster for many individuals. In each of these cases, it's not choosing between allowing your time to be wasted or not allowing it—it's a case of choosing between allowing your time to be wasted or achieving success. As Charles Darwin said: *A man who dares waste one hour of life has not discovered the value of life.*

Another type of Time Bandit is the individual who wants you to do what he or she wants instead of what you want, or instead of what you *should* do to achieve your goals. These Time Bandits say things like, "Let's take a run to the mall," when you want to work toward one of your goals. They hang around your desk when you have important assignments to work on. They call when you're doing your studying and say, "You can study later, let's go out."

It is amazing that we let Time Bandits decide how to spend our time, but we do. We wouldn't let someone spend our money, but we'll allow someone to spend our time, which is far more valuable. Because your time is literally your life, if you let Time Bandits have their way, they are going to live two lives, yours and theirs—and you won't have lived either of them.

> *Time is the one thing that can never be re-trieved. One may lose and regain a friend; one may lose and regain money; opportunity once spurned may come again; but the hours lost in idleness can never be brought back to be used in gainful purposes.*
>
> —C. R. Lawton

Time Bandits are not just individuals, they can be organizations, events, and circumstances as well. Every commitment you make to join an organization, every responsibility you accept, every invitation you accept, and every magazine subscription you order is going to spend your time for you. If that coincides with your choices, fine; but if not, you need to cancel the subscription, decline the invitation, or drop out of the group—tough choices, but they must be made if you really want to be successful and in total control of your life.

The only effective techniques I know of for dealing with Time Bandit Anacondas are to consciously choose to do something else and acquire a new habit to do it—like getting into the habit of reading instead of watching television, and to do this: SAY NO. I put it in capital letters because I think that is the way it should be done—not in a nasty way, but firmly, so your "no" sticks, whether you say it to an individual or to yourself.

Saying no is difficult for most individuals because most of us are in the *habit* of going along— going along with how someone else wants to spend our time. If this sounds familiar to you, you must exchange your going-along habit for the habit of spending time according to your priorities and your plans.

Time Bandits steal away more than your time because along with your time goes your energy and your enthusiasm to pursue other things. This results in *diffusion*. Diffusion is rarely productive—what you must do is conserve and concentrate your energies and enthusiasm on the goals that are important to you.

In Sum . . .

♦ Time Bandit Anacondas take your time and make it their own; they spend your time on activities that are not your priorities to success. The goal is to consciously spend your time as you choose.

♦ Learn to say *NO!*

The Worst Anaconda Of Them All

Are you ready for this? The worst Anaconda of them all, the one that does the most damage, the one that is the most deadly by far . . . can be yourself!

You are your own worst Anaconda when your self-talk is negative or *can't* oriented, when you allow yourself to hold mental images of what you don't want to happen, and when your vision of yourself is a you with less than you deserve.

> *I can. It is a powerful sentence. I can.*
> —Og Mandino

When you say things like *what a lousy week it's been,* you might just as well have stabbed the positive *you* in the left ventricle. And when you say things like *I can't lose weight, why bother, who cares, I'll never be rich, I'm not lucky,* or *I'll never be anything but a* whatever, you are winding your Dream-Snatching coils around your soul and crushing it dead, dead, dead. When you talk to yourself with phrases like *I'm not good at chemistry,* or *I'm timid,* or *I'm tired all the time,* you are committing yourself to those images. As Marilyn Grey puts it: *Your brain doesn't know you're kidding. Random thoughts such as . . . "This job makes me sick" are viewed by the right brain as instructions.*

There is only one person responsible for you: You. And if you are out of control, then you'd better speak to the person in charge—that's you, too! This means you are also responsible for the Anaconda in you. To begin to deal with your Anaconda-self, you must develop good self-talk and imaging habits.

In Sum . . .

♦ *You* can be your own worst Anaconda, and you must control yourself through positive self-talk and positive imaging.

Obstacles are like wild animals. They are cowards but they will bluff you if they can. If they see you are afraid of them . . . they are liable to spring upon you; but . . . if you look them squarely in the eye, they will slink out of sight.

—Orison Swett Marden

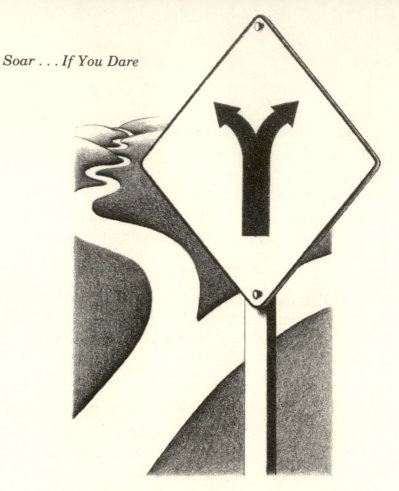

The Anacondas In Life
What To Do . . .

1. Be on the lookout for the Anacondas in your life and when you see or hear them coming, avoid them if you can; and if you can't, stop and think. Use your power of choice to consciously refuse them your dreams and reject their limiting thoughts.

2. Get into the habit of changing conversation from negative to positive—from can't-do to can-do.

3. When confronted with a Dream Snatcher you can't avoid:

   Assess the source, realizing that no one has all the answers or can predict or create your future better than you.

   Get the facts and experience necessary to make your own choices—talk to others in the field, do your own research, make your own evaluation.

   Begin immediately to create and reinforce your belief in your dreams by transforming them into a plan that you can follow to bring them about.

   Use your power of imagination and begin creating and repeating in your mind pictures of your dreams becoming a reality.

4. Eliminate doubt, despair, and other limitations from your mind. Bolster your belief with positive, affirming self-talk.

5. Recognize that you deserve the very best in life and you can have it—no one sat in judgment to decide what you deserve—you get to decide.

6. Don't put any limitations on yourself or in your mind.

7. Avoid the Time Bandits in life. Learn to say NO. Choose to spend your time the way you want to.

8. Control your thoughts through positive self-talk and positive imaging.

*Your only
limitations are
those you set up
in your mind,
or permit
others to set up
for you!*

—Og Mandino

Three

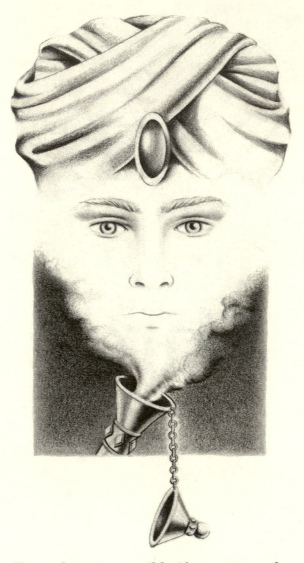

*Everything is possible if you can truly
believe . . . if you can truly believe in your
subconscious mind, that is.*

Genie Power!

ABU is the street thief in *The Thief Of Baghdad* who is plagued with one dilemma after another. Nothing is going right it seems and as Abu strolls along the seashore contemplating his difficulties, he catches a glimpse of an odd bottle washed up on the sand.

Abu dashes to the bottle and twists out the cork releasing a whooshing cloud of smoke. Abu yelps and falls backwards in the sand while cowering and looking skyward at the genie forming before him.

"Don't be afraid," the genie says. "I'm not here to harm you. In fact, because you have released me, I will grant any three wishes you may wish, Master."

Master? Abu thinks to himself. Did he say Master? Hmmm.

"You're not afraid of me are you, little friend?" the genie asks. He laughs. "Or perhaps you don't believe I can grant your wishes."

Although skeptical and certainly still intimidated, Abu doesn't want to miss the chance of a lifetime and he certainly doesn't want the giant genie to know that he was afraid only a moment ago. So Abu stands and says: "No, I am not afraid of you, and of course I believe you can grant my wishes, I am just thinking about them".

As he contemplates further, Abu feels the pangs of hunger in his stomach and he thinks to himself that he would be able to figure out this situation better if he just had something to eat. Without realizing it, he mumbles out loud: "I wish I had some sausages to eat."

Snap! The genie lowers his giant palm to reveal a frying pan of sizzling sausages. "Your wish is my command, Master," the genie says. "Your sausages."

Now, you may be thinking that there are no magic genies and that this has nothing to do with you. Please withhold your final judgment, for I am about to explain how we each can make our wishes come true if we will only learn how to believe in our own personal Genie Power and summon it at will to our command.

We each have Genie Power and we can use it to get whatever we want. Our Genie Power is our ability to create or change our beliefs within our subconscious minds. Let me repeat that because it is so important. You have Genie Power—the ability to change the innermost beliefs deep within your subconscious mind. Regardless of what your beliefs may now be, regardless of how long you have had them, regardless of anything else on this earth, you can change what you believe.

Like Abu in the story, if we do not believe we can get what we wish for, we won't wish for it and we won't get it. But if we do believe, well then, we can get whatever we want.

The beliefs within our subconscious minds establish the boundaries and limitations of our goals, self-esteem, personal deservedness, capabilities, and other factors. We can crash through these barriers to get what we want in life only by first altering our existing subconscious beliefs or by creating new ones—and it is only through the control and management of our subconscious minds that we can make such changes.

> *You cannot fathom your mind. The more you draw from it, the more clear and fruitful it will be.*
> —George A. Sala

Many individuals have written or spoken about the unique ability that each of us has to control the beliefs we have in our subconscious minds. In his book, *The Power of Your Subconscious Mind*, Joseph Murphy wrote: *The law of life is the law of belief, and belief could be summed up briefly as a thought in your mind.* Norman Vincent Peale referred to the critical importance of this exceptional force in *The Power of Positive Thinking* when he wrote: *To learn to believe is of primary importance. It is the basic factor of succeeding in any undertaking.* Napoleon Hill referred to it in *Think And Grow Rich* when he wrote: *What the mind of man can conceive and believe, the mind of man can achieve.* And Claude M. Bristol put it this way in *The Magic of Believing*: *Just believe that there is a genuine creative magic in believing—and magic there will be, for belief will supply the power which will enable you to succeed in everything you undertake. Begin your belief with a resolute will and you become unconquerable—a master among men—yourself.*

In Sum . . .

♦ Belief, deep within our subconscious minds, is an absolute requirement for the achievement of our goals.

♦ Genie Power is a unique power each of us has to alter what we believe deep within our subconscious minds—we can use Genie Power to create belief if we don't already have it, or to change what we believe at our will.

How Do You Create Belief If It Doesn't Already Exist?

Every religion known to man is founded upon the principles of belief. Every great or small accomplishment in life has been achieved because someone or some group of people *believed* it could be achieved.

If thou canst believe, all things are possible to him that believeth.

—Mark:9:23

But belief itself is not always easy. Note that Mark's verse in the Bible begins, *If thou canst believe.* This certainly is a tip-off that just getting to the state of belief may be the first obstacle we have to overcome; similarly, to have to change our beliefs is often an obstacle as well.

Unfortunately, we can't all of a sudden believe something or change our beliefs about something just because we want to. What is required is what Dr. Peale said we must do: We must "learn to believe." Fortunately, you can learn how to believe things you don't already believe and you can learn to change your existing beliefs by mastering certain techniques.

For example, let's say that you want a better job, but that you don't truly believe you can get one. Maybe you tell yourself consciously that you believe you can get a better job, but somewhere deep down inside is a little doubt that nags at you every now and then. Perhaps you don't acknowledge this doubt outright, but in your heart of hearts, you know it is there. So, in reality, you don't truly believe—not 100 percent anyway. Now, how do you get such belief if you don't have it? *That* is the question.

> *The mind is the limit. As long as the mind can envision the fact that you can do something, you can do it—as long as you really believe 100 percent.*
> —Arnold Schwarzenegger

The answer to getting to a state of belief is to use Genie Power. What that means is to allow yourself to do what you so naturally do when you watch movies like the *Thief Of Baghdad*. The way to create belief if it doesn't already exist is this: *pretend.*

It is easy to understand the concept of Abu's genie and the power of his genie because we can all pretend and imagine a giant genie on the beach and easily go along with the genie's magic creation of pulling a pan of sizzling sausages out of thin air. It is effortless for us to imagine and believe this on a pretend basis in our minds without having our intellect get in the way. Child's play. We just click off all the intellectual reasoning in our brains, put all logic on hold, and say to ourselves, okay, let's pretend. The moment we do that, a whole new dimension in our thinking opens up, and at least on a pretend basis, *anything is possible!*

This anything-is-possible phenomenon is exactly what occurs each time we walk into a movie theater. We click off reality and allow ourselves the child's play of *entering* and believing unquestioningly a whole new world. When we watched *Star Wars, ET, The Terminator, Big, Honey I Shrunk the Kids*, or any other movie, for that matter, we didn't sit there eating popcorn while thinking "none of this is possible" or "I don't believe it." Instead, we were there. We allowed our magic minds to pretend—to believe, at least for a hundred and twenty minutes or so, that what we were seeing and hearing was real. The same thing happens when we read a good book or listen to or tell a good story. We enter a new world and while we are there it is not life-like—it is our life.

We think to ourselves "this is ridiculous" in only a few instances: when the movie is made poorly, when the "set up" of the fantasy is not established right away, and when there are distractions to our trains of thought. In other words, we will allow ourselves to enter a pretend world of fantasy only when "it" is done right. Only when it is a great, well-written book, only when it is a great, well-made movie, and only when we can get absorbed into the medium without distractions will we allow ourselves to pretend. But when these conditions exist, we enter a whole new world of belief that is just as real as though we existed in it in the physical sense.

> *In using your subconscious mind . . . infer no opponent, . . . use no will power . . . imagine the end. You will find your intellect trying to get in the way, but persist in maintaining a simple, child-like, miracle-making faith.*
> —Joseph Murphy

The obstacle to changing our beliefs is our own intellect, our intellect is the Anaconda obstacle within our minds. When we try to dream, it is a natural tendency to apply our logic and reasoning to our thoughts and to test and validate what we are thinking by recollecting all the memories of what we have been told and of what we have experienced. We apply our intellect in this manner and in no time at all we have rationalized ourselves right out of our ability to believe in our own dreams. The more we try to reason with ourselves, the more we lose this battle. We can't fight our own intellect and win because it is a combat with ourselves. So what we must do is avoid our intellect and our reasoning, and we can do this easily by pretending.

Genie Power, then, is our ability to change what we believe and we put it in motion by pretending. Simply put: Genie Power is pretending.

The reason Genie Power works is because when you acknowledge to yourself consciously that you are pretending, you then release your mind of all pre-existing restrictions and allow it to run with the wind without preconceived biases. You give yourself the opportunity to begin thinking with a fresh sheet of paper before you, so to speak. No preconceptions. Nothing on the page except what you want to put there. No limitations.

Faith is to believe what we do not see; and the reward of this faith is to see what we believe.
—St. Augustine

To apply the concept of Genie Power to the get-a-better-job example, what you could do is be honest with yourself and say, "Okay, so maybe I don't really believe I can get a better job, but what I'm going to do is allow myself to daydream, to pretend that I can get one." You would then pretend, perhaps by saying: "Now, let me see, if I *were* going to get a better job, the first thing I might do is decide what my strengths are and what I like to do, then what I probably would do is update my resume listing my accomplishments and highlighting my strengths, and then . . ." You would continue this process all the while pretending and imagining all the things you *might* do.

What is interesting is that in pretending like this, what you are doing in actuality is figuring out how you would go about changing jobs. And once you have figured out how to change jobs, even if only on a pretend basis, this new knowledge becomes a part of your intellect and it will begin like magic to actually change your belief about whether you can change jobs. Explained another way, by pretending, you reasoned in your mind how you *might* change jobs, and this added reasoning and logic provide a whole new basis for your beliefs. This doesn't happen overnight, of course, but if applied on a sustained basis, your logic and knowledge would indeed change.

Take another example. Let's say you want to get into the habit of spending a little time each night reading a book versus watching TV. And let's say that deep down inside you know that it is not like you to do this because you are a lifelong couch potato, and you don't truly believe this is possible.

Here again, what you could do is pretend that you are an avid reader, reading a little each night. You could begin by imagining yourself going to the library, determining the kinds of books you like, making your selections, getting into a comfortable chair to read your books and so on. You *could* imagine all of these things on a pretend basis, and if you do this, and if you get disciplined about it and do it often enough in imaginary detail, then sooner or later you will begin to change your view of yourself and your subconscious beliefs.

> *Believing is drawing a mental blueprint, and, when you accomplish that, the word "impossible" is eliminated from your thinking.*
>
> —Charles L. Allen

You can't change your beliefs about anything, however, unless you are prepared to reinforce your pretending with your actions. This is critical, for any hesitation to act on your part will be interpreted as doubt, and it will be the doubt that gets acted upon by your subconscious mind. Actions impact thoughts and emotions, which in turn impact actions. This cycle is a never-ending chain of thought-action-thought, and action is an essential link in the process. Everything falls apart if your actions don't reinforce your thoughts. You can't truly begin to establish belief until you take action as though what you believed in was already so or at least in the process of becoming so.

*What goal would you pursue if you knew it
was impossible to fail?*
                                    —Robert Schuller

To create true belief, it sometimes is more a
matter of removing all doubt than it is of establishing
belief. To remove doubt, it often is necessary to take
the bold, unhesitating actions you would take if you
were absolutely certain you could not possibly fail for
any reason whatsoever.

One example is the time I wanted a promotion
and a raise. I went out and bought new suits in ex-
pectation of getting both the raise and the promotion.
Wearing the new suits made me feel, look, and act
confident. The result was that I got my raise and my
promotion. Yes, I had done a lot of good work leading
up to this, but I'm convinced that any lack of confidence on my part could have resulted in a far different
outcome. So to avoid doubting myself, I bought the
suits. I took action.

An even bigger example of this from my own life
is when I decided to leave the sixteen-year career I
had had in public accounting. My first action was to
resign, even before I had a new career lined up. It was
like burning the ships in the harbor, but that action
actually had the effect of bolstering my confidence
and belief that I would be successful in my new
career, which I was.

While I don't necessarily recommend that everyone who wants to change jobs run right out and quit their present one, I do think that if you want to change jobs and get yourself into a state of believing that it will happen, then you must begin to take some actions. Perhaps you would put your resume together. Maybe you would attend a seminar or two to expand your network of contacts.

The precise actions you take are not as important as that you take some. Taking actions to create belief is a little understood phenomenon, but it works. Ask yourself what actions you would take if it were impossible for you to fail. Whatever they are, start doing them, for they will bolster your belief and drive you toward the successes you desire.

When you begin to develop your dreams and take steps to believe in them, make them big dreams for big things, for it is big dreams for big things that will give you big power. As Dr. David J. Schwartz stresses in his book *The Magic Of Thinking Big: Big ideas and big plans are often easier—certainly no more difficult—than small ideas and small plans.*

Think BIG. Dream BIG. Act BIG. On your next birthday when you close your eyes to blow out the candles on your cake, make a real wish, and make it big. If you are like Abu and use your wish only for sausages, that's what you will get.

Someone once said that we have to *throw our hearts over the fence so our bodies will follow*. There is a lot of truth in this because this is rekindling your ability to have faith in your dreams, like you did as a child. It is allowing yourself to pretend and to dream. The other side of this, of course, is that if we throw our bodies over the fence, our hearts would have little choice but to follow. And this is the action part of pretending and changing our beliefs. We must take actions to bolster our beliefs in our dreams.

In Sum . . .

♦ To create a belief that you don't already have, learn to be a child again and dream. Allow yourself to believe in your dreams in a pretend way.

♦ Pretending will change your knowledge, and this will alter your belief.

♦ Reinforce your thoughts about what you want to believe with actions.

♦ Think BIG. Dream BIG. Act BIG.

Pulling the Cork From the Bottle

Reader's Digest reported a quip about a young shoe salesman who kept a badge pinned to his shirt that read: *If you forgot your smile today, I'll lend you mine.*

This has a lot to do with Genie Power because it has to do with releasing a positive attitude on a daily basis, which is like pulling the cork from the bottle every day. Here is one reason this is important: I have never met a negative person who was a true dreamer and I have never met a positive person who wasn't. Never.

Your attitude is your *feeling toward a fact or a condition*. It's not the actual fact or condition that's important—rather, it's your feeling toward it. It's not what's going on around you that's the key—it's what's going on inside your head. Your attitude is not determined by the Anacondas in life and what they say or do—your attitude is determined by what *you* think, say, and do in response.

It is important to note that although your attitude is affected by what you think, it also is affected by what you *say* and *do*; often, what you say and do will have a bigger impact on your attitude than just your thoughts.

The example of the young shoe salesman with his smiling badge points out that we don't have to go through life waiting for something to react to so we can decide what our attitude will be toward it. Instead, like the shoe salesman, we can decide *in advance* what our attitude will be. We can decide to always have a smile, to always have a good word to say, to always look for the positive. These are choices we can make and we should make.

Each day of your life, as soon as you open your eyes in the morning, you can square away for a happy and successful day. It's the mood and the purpose at the inception of each day that are the important facts in charting your course for the day. We can always square away for a fresh start, no matter what the past has been. It's today that is the paramount problem always. Yesterday is but history.

—George Matthew Adams

If an Anaconda is trying to snatch a dream from you, or is threatening your plans, just the simple *acts* of maintaining an erect posture and a smile often will be enough to maintain your positive attitude toward your dream. Imagine that. A simple smile and an erect posture can make you impervious—not only to the little obstacles in life, but also to the big ones.

But the moment you slump your shoulders or begin to nod agreement with the Anaconda Dream Snatcher or the Anaconda of Doubt, then that is the precise moment your dream begins to slip away. For this reason, positive *reaction* reflexes must become *habits,* and this often means that you have to exchange a negative reaction habit that you already have for a positive reaction habit that you need to acquire in its place.

Eleanor Roosevelt said: *No one can make you feel*

inferior without your consent. Extending this thought, *no one can steal your dreams without your consent.* We all need to get into the habit of refusing others our dreams. And we need to do so because there simply are so many Anaconda Dream Snatchers around. Richard N. Bolles, author of *What Color Is Your Parachute?*, puts it this way: *One of the saddest lines in the world is 'oh come now—be realistic.' The best parts of the world were not fashioned by those who were realistic. They were fashioned by those who dared to look hard at their wishes and gave them horses to ride.*

There you have it. Dare to dream, and dare to hold on to your dreams. There is not a person or thing on earth that can get inside your head to snatch away a single thought, or plant a single seed of doubt unless you let them. Keep your dreams, and keep a positive attitude toward your dreams by developing the habit of positive *reaction* reflexes.

> *Hold fast to dreams*
> *For if dreams die*
> *Life is a broken-winged bird*
> *That cannot fly.*
> *Hold fast to your dreams*
> *For when dreams go*
> *Life is a barren field*
> *Frozen with snow.*
> —Langston Hughes

It is wise to keep your dreams to yourself, or at least to confine knowledge of them to a small group of people—individuals you know for certain are not Dream Snatchers. The reason is simple. Dream Snatchers can't snatch your dreams if they don't know what your dreams are. Napoleon Hill offered similar advice when he recommended the sharing of dreams and plans only with a *Mastermind Group,* a small group of people you trust totally, a group that emphatically believes in you, a group that wants you to succeed.

If you don't have a Mastermind Group in your life, you can create one in your mind, and it can include people like Winston Churchill, Confucius, Eleanor Roosevelt, even Jesus or the god of your choosing. All you have to do is imagine meeting with these individuals and asking their advice, then imagine what they would say to you. This may sound hokey at first, but I assure you it isn't. Your mind has the capacity to create all of this to use to your advantage, just as though your Mastermind Group were alive and meeting in your living room. The results from this technique will be nothing short of amazing.

In Sum . . .

♦ The Anacondas in life are out to get your dreams and they will, unless you fight them off.

♦ You can change your feelings and you can change your attitude, and a positive attitude is sufficient to fend off any Anaconda that comes your way.

♦ To always have a positive attitude, get into the habit of having positive action reflexes.

♦ Share your dreams only with those close to you who you are certain are not Dream Snatchers.

Be A Dream Sower

The good news is that not everyone is a Dream Snatcher and all Dream Snatchers do not always snatch dreams away. Often many of these same people are *Dream Sowers*.

A demonstration of a Dream Sower using even a seemingly minor stimulus is Mike Vance's story, which I heard him relate in person.

Vance, who was the dean of Disney University, attributes the impetus for his own creativity to a childhood experience. One day when Mike was a boy, he went to visit his neighbor, a man named Adam Earhart, but his neighbor wasn't home. Mike wanted him to know he had been there, so he spelled his name out in sticks that he gathered from the yard. Later, Mike was upstairs at home when Mr. Earhart came over and said to his mother: "Isn't Mike creative? He decided to leave me a calling card spelling out his name with sticks when he found out I wasn't home today."

Isn't Mike creative? That was all it took. From that point on, Mike Vance thought of himself as creative, and indeed today he is. His neighbor was a Dream Sower. He planted the seed for Mike's creativity and it grew.

You can be a Dream Sower, too, for yourself as well as for others. Good or bad, positive or not, thought seeds do grow. This is why it is so critical for parents and teachers to be planting positive seeds in the minds of children. Positive thought seeds planted in any mind have a good chance to grow. But in the minds of children, they can be unstoppable because their mind gardens are just beginning.

It's what each of us sows, and how, that gives us character and prestige. Seeds of kindness, goodwill, and human understanding, planted in fertile soil, spring up into death-less friendship, big deeds of worth, and a memory that will not soon fade out. We are all sowers of seeds—and let us never forget it!
—George Matthew Adams

Someone offered me this advice when my two daughters were still truly my little girls: "When you kiss them goodnight, hug them and whisper 'you're terrific, I love you.'" I took that advice only I added these words: "And you're so creative, I'm so proud of you." Now, guess what? Both my daughters consider themselves creative, very creative in fact—and you know what? They are. Because of a few simple seeds planted with hugs.

In Sum . . .

◆ You can be a Dream Sower.

Follow these four steps:

> *First, THINK*
> *Second, BELIEVE*
> *Third, DREAM*
> *And finally, DARE.*
>
> — Walt Disney's advice to an
> eight-year-old who wanted
> to grow up to be like
> Disney himself.

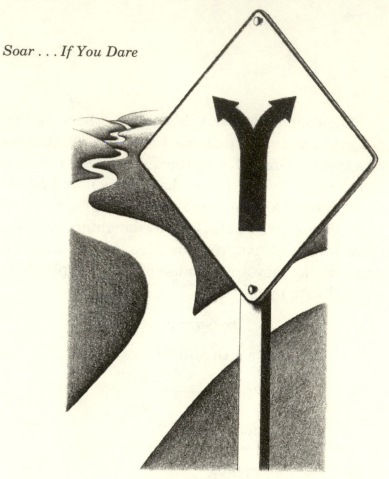

Genie Power!
What To Do . . .

1. Create and repeatedly hold images in your mind of what you want to believe—let yourself pretend.

2. Have faith in your dreams and immediately set forth to develop plans to achieve them. Do this even if you have a lingering doubt about what you really believe.

3. Begin taking the actions *you would imagine taking* if you knew you could not fail.

4. Think BIG. Dream BIG. Act BIG.

5. Keep your dreams to yourself or share them only with a few individuals who believe in you—those individuals can be a handful of friends you create only in your mind.

6. Decide what your attitude will be and make it positive. Get into the habit of having positive reaction reflexes to all the Anacondas in life.

7. Be a Dream Sower for others—plant positive thought seeds—they will grow.

*There is
nothing on
earth that you
can not
have—once you
have mentally
accepted the
fact that you
can have it.*
—Robert Collier

Four

*You hold the magical key to all that you
want in the universe and it is this: You
alone make all the choices in your life
and in making these choices you
determine what you become.*

The Power Of Your Choices

OG MANDINO pointed out in *The Choice* that millions and millions of unhappy people *have never exercised their options for the better things in life because they have never been aware they have choice.* This would be like sitting in front of a blank television screen and not using the remote control in your hand to select a channel because you didn't know what the remote control was.

Yet for millions of people, that is precisely what occurs when it comes to the major choices in life. It seems everyone can make the "flavor" choices in life, like making selections from a menu in a restaurant, deciding what style of clothes to buy or picking what kind of car to own. The breakdowns occur with the more important choices in life: the menus are there, but people choose not to see them, or they narrow their menus down to simple selections. They choose not to choose.

In Sum . . .

◆ Many people have not exercised their options for the better things in life because they are not aware that they have choice.

The Mortal Choices In Life: What Will You Be? What Will You Do?

Most individuals haven't given a half-hour's uninterrupted thought to deciding or even thinking about what they will be or what they will do, yet these are two of the most significant choices we each have.

If you don't know what you want in life, a terrible thing happens—NOTHING!

What is riveting once you think about it is that the Power of Choice is much more than just the ability to choose what you will become and what you will do—*the act of choosing itself creates the power* to become what you want to become and do what you want to do. Making a choice actually gives you the power.

This may read like an illusion in logic at first, but the act of choosing literally flips the ignition switch to your internal power, thus launching your actions and emotions toward the goals you have chosen.

As Gloria Estephan belts out repeatedly in her popular song: *We seal our fate with the choices we make.*

When you think through your options and say to yourself, yes, I want to go to college and graduate, you put into motion all sorts of thoughts within your mind, and these immediately begin to manifest themselves in your outward actions. You start telling people you are going to college, you start being more observant of what you read and hear about colleges you may be considering. But none or very little of this happens until you actually make the choice.

> *The objective in life is to choose the right goals, and then to cause to occur that which must take place to achieve them.*
> — Unknown

The act of choosing is the event that sets things in motion. Without this event, everything languishes and our inner energy remains at a standstill. This is true of the little things in our lives as well as the big ones.

When we decide to have a pizza brought in for dinner, it is only after this choice is made that someone makes the call—no one goes near the phone until a decision is made. This may seem a trivial example, but the underlying principle is not—the secret power of choices—*the act of choosing* puts things in motion.

When you click the remote control to your television and turn the set on and select a channel, in the words of Flip Wilson, *what you see is what you get*. Life works the same way—when you make a choice, that is what you will get, and when you make a choice, it is then and only then that you will begin to move toward your goal.

In Sum . . .

♦ Your two mortal choices in life are:
  What will you be?
  What will you do?

♦ The *power of choice* is choosing what you will become, but it also starts creating what you will become.

Tombstone Choices And The Man With A Twang Who Can Change Your Life

I was in my mid thirties before I understood the true meaning and importance of the power of choice. Arriving at a seminar in October 1983, I found an out-of-the-way side seat and sat back sipping my coffee. I was prepared to be bored and wished I had ditched the seminar because I had so much to do at the office. The hundred or so other attendees were shuffling to their seats when in strolled a tall fellow with silver hair. His "good morning y'all" twang was more bubbly than I wanted to hear right then. I mumbled some unpleasantry as I stretched up in my seat to see if he was wearing cowboy boots, which he was, as I recall. He also was wearing a string tie, I believe, but I must admit this occurred years ago and I've told this story so many times (embellishing as I go along, of course) that I'm no longer sure of what is fact and what isn't. But I do assure you that the gist of this is true to the bone.

Anyway, the man introduced himself as Lewis Timberlake of Austin, Texas. He entertained us non-stop for two hours with anecdote-filled recommendations about making the most of our lives. I was paying attention and taking notes when unbeknownst to me (at the time) Lewis Timberlake hauled off and hit me right between the eyes so hard with what he said that he could just as well have used a two-by-four and had

81

the same impact—it was several days later before I realized I had been struck.

Lewis Timberlake challenged us to plan our lives by starting at our life's end—by going home and writing our epitaph, one to be read by those left behind at the time of death, hopefully at some long-distant date.

Timberlake instructed us to write one sentence in our epitaphs for each of the six different components of our lives: 1) our spiritual lives, 2) our family lives, 3) our mental lives, 4) our physical lives, 5) our social lives, and 6) our career/financial lives. He told us to imagine a loved one reading these six lines of our epitaphs on the headstones of our graves.

Timberlake guessed that only one or two people in our group would actually go home and write their epitaphs, but he promised that anyone who did could expect to have a dramatic and positive change in their life within six months.

Two nights later I poured myself some sipping whiskey, and I sat down to begin the task. When I got to the sentence in my epitaph about my career, I pondered for a while and reflected on where I was headed. At the time I was the partner-in-charge of a rapidly growing office in one of the Big Eight (now Big Six) public accounting firms.

In thinking through my epitaph, I decided that at my career's end I would be the managing partner of a much larger office in that firm. I wrote that down on paper. Then I imagined my two daughters standing at my headstone, reading the words *I myself had selected* to describe what I had done with the only life I had to live. The disappointment I felt at that moment is impossible to relate fully, but I can tell you that it shivered across my shoulders and shot down my back. Is that it? I said aloud. I had always thought of myself as a creator of things—an idea man—well what and where are the things you created? I asked myself. Surely you could have accomplished more.

I balled up my first epitaph attempt, flipped it towards the basket and on a fresh sheet of paper began a new one. I decided to elevate my position substantially, and I wrote down that I had become the managing partner of the entire firm, the chief executive officer—making oodles of money, of course. I splurged and expanded my allotted single epitaph sentence to two lines and explained how the firm had tripled in size under my leadership.

Then I sat back, sipped my whiskey, and again imagined my two daughters reading the chiseled words in polished granite.

I got a nauseating cold rush and I sensed that it wasn't just a feeling that had passed through me, but my life itself. Then bam! It hit me—I felt like there was suddenly a wooden stake being pounded into my heart, and I knew I was burning daylight.

For the very *first* time in my life I understood that I had *choice,* and yet I was spending the only life I had to live in a career that wasn't my career of choice. The revelation was so clear to me then and there that I had been relentlessly pursuing a career that was not a choice I had made, but instead was one I had stumbled into by happenstance.

I didn't know in that instant what I would become or what I would do, but I understood in a flash that what I was doing wasn't going to get me where I wanted to go, wherever that was. I finished my sipping whiskey, and two weeks later I resigned my position.

> *In the long run you hit only what you aim at*
> *. . . aim at something high.*
> —Henry David Thoreau

People have asked me whether it was hard to decide to leave the firm I was with. After all, sixteen years is a long time. The company was like a womb for me—it was the only place I had worked since college.

The answer is no. While implementing my choice was another matter, *making* the choice to leave was easy. I *had* to move on.

I don't mean to imply that I knew right then and there exactly what I wanted to do in life career-wise, because I didn't. That took some time to figure out.

But I did know I was not on the right path. I knew I was going in a direction that wasn't right for me.

Being a partner with a big accounting firm is a fine career, and it wasn't the career that was wrong. It was me in that career that was wrong—I wanted to choose something different. I never realized until that evening that I was the one who actually gets to make the choice.

> *Many of us are like the little boy we met trudging along a country road with a cat-rifle over his shoulder. "What are you hunting buddy," we asked. "Dunno, sir, I ain't seen it yet."*
>
> — Unknown

One of the more important parts of my "tombstone planning" exercise, as I call it, was forcing myself to reduce my envisioned epitaph to writing. Another important part was imagining my daughters standing at my headstone reading what I had written. Successful or not in achieving my tombstone choices, more than anything I wanted to be remembered for having made good choices, choices my children would understand and be proud of.

> *I am the master of my fate: I am the captain of my soul.*
>
> —From *Invictus*
> by William Ernest Henley

What will you be? What will you do?—These are your choices. Your life will be changed when you make them, I promise you that. Your tombstone choices are tremendous keys to your universe, and the power they can unleash is enough to move any mountains that may get in your way.

Don't let someone else decide for you what the world will read on your tombstone. Decide for yourself. Choose your own epitaph. Write it out now and know that it will change your life; and when your life changes, don't thank me, drop Lewis Timberlake a note at: P.O. Box 1571, Austin, Texas, 78767.

In Sum . . .

♦ Your tombstone choices represent what you wish to be remembered for in each of the six components of your life: spiritual; family; mental; physical; social; career/financial.

Goal Choices—The Ends Or The Means?

In addition to the big choices you make in life— the mortal ones that will be reflected on your tombstone—the goals you choose are important, too. Goals are the ends toward which you direct your efforts, but more importantly than just serving as targets, goals are the magnets necessary to pull you along your way.

The specific nature of your goals is important, but more significant is that you have taken the time to specify them and adopt them as your goals in the first place. As Geoffry F. Abert put it: *The most important thing about goals is having one.*

There is no progress without goals. Like the carrot in front of the donkey pulling the cart, *goals release the power and the motivation for our forward actions and thoughts.* But, goals can't release this power until you choose them.

Many individuals see goals only as desired results being pursued. What they overlook is the more important aspect of goals: *Goals are choices and as choices they are the means to results.* Ben Stein wrote: *The indispensable first step to getting the things you want out of life is this: decide what you want.*

Deciding isn't just any step toward getting what you want—it is the *first* step and it *must* occur before any other steps can follow. When you get into a taxi, the driver doesn't step on the gas until you tell the driver where you have decided to go. After you say, "Take me to the airport," then the cabby steps on it. This works the same in all of your experiences. When you decide what you want, you engage the driving force in your life and the source of your power. All of your thoughts and actions are born and driven toward their goals only after you have chosen what those goals will be.

What is remarkable is that you literally begin to move toward the achievement of your goals the instant you establish them. The moment you decide to get something to eat, your body begins to secrete digestive fluids in anticipation of the process that follows eating. This is a rudimentary example of the power of expectancy, a well-established concept that results follow from establishing a vivid goal. But everything else we do works the same way, provided our goals are well-defined.

You will know your goals are complete and working to your advantage when they possess these elements:

Goals must be:
1. WRITTEN
2. VISUAL
3. PRIORITIZED
4. SPECIFIC

Goals must have:

5. DEADLINES
6. COMMITMENTS
7. PLANS

Many individuals see their goals end up on a pile of passing fantasies because they were incomplete in one or more of the listed ways. You will have an excellent chance of achieving each of your goals if they possess these seven basic elements.

> *Since the mind is a specific biocomputer, it needs specific instructions and directions. The reason most people never reach their goals is that they don't define them, learn about them, or ever seriously consider them as believable or achievable. Winners can tell you where they are going, what they plan to do along the way, and who will be sharing the adventure with them.*
>
> —Denis Waitley

I have heard many individuals say that they really don't need to write down their goals or their plans to achieve them. Although there is no way to prove this point beyond a shadow of doubt, I can tell you from experience that the simple act of writing out goals and the plans to achieve them is enormously energizing. The power of writing down your choices is mysterious, yet I believe it is undeniable.

Writing down your goals and your choices is the first tangible evidence that you have begun to transform a thought into a physical reality. It is precisely this transformation process that is absolutely necessary for results to be achieved.

To maximize the magical and magnetic power of goals in pulling you toward results that you desire, you should always be able to answer these questions:

> What are the three primary goals you are pursuing right now? Name them in the order of their priority.

> When will each of your goals be achieved and what are your plans to achieve them?

> What did you do TODAY to advance you toward your goals? What will you do TOMORROW? And what will you do NEXT WEEK and NEXT MONTH?

In the context of the questions above, goals are not to be confused with milestones you are pursuing, interim steps along the way, or such things as daily "to do" items. Each of these is an excellent tool to help maintain progress and your personal effectiveness, but goals are different. Goals are usually bigger in scope than each of these other items, and goals always should possess the seven elements mentioned earlier.

For example, I have thirty or so items on my to

do listing covering the next few weeks, but in reality I only have three major goals I am pursuing right now. One of these goals, for example, is to get this book finished and to the market for the Christmas season. This goal meets all seven criteria: it is written; it is visual—I see the books being purchased and read and given as gifts; it is prioritized as my most important goal until it is completed; it is very specific; the deadlines are set; I am committed to this; and I have a plan to achieve this goal. I do have additional goals beyond the three I am pursuing now, quite a few in fact, the only difference is that they are on my agenda to begin in a few months. I recognize that I can't pursue them all at once and expect to make real progress toward any one of them, so I prioritized—prioritization is the third element of a goal.

What goals are you pursuing right now? Can you name them? Did you do something today to move you closer to achieving your goals? Do you have something planned to move you closer still tomorrow? And next week? If you can't name your goals and the steps you are taking to achieve them, it almost is a certainty that you are risking achieving them at all, or that your progress is much less than it could be. Why risk accomplishing your goals, and why not achieve your goals as soon as you can?

Let's say you are a student. Perhaps one of your primary near-term goals is to be hired by a great firm upon graduation. A corollary goal might be getting terrific grades this semester, perhaps straight As. If asked, most students probably would agree that they have goals something like these, but how many students have gone to the trouble to write their goals down, visualize them, prioritize them, set deadlines for them, develop specific plans for them and so on. Very few, but the few who do, have a far better chance of achieving their goals than those individuals who don't.

Or let's say you are not happily employed and that you would like to change jobs. Well, what is your goal exactly? To change jobs within the same firm, to change firms, or to change both? When exactly do you want to have this goal achieved? What's your plan? What did you do today that brought you closer to achieving your goal? What's on your agenda for tomorrow?

I'm sure you see the point. If you are not working on hitting one of your targets, it's going to be hard to score a bull's eye. There is an enormous difference between really, truly having goals and not having them, but while allowing yourself to pretend that you do.

Having true, honest-to-goodness goals meeting all seven criteria is one of the secrets of success in whatever you are trying to accomplish. If you want to lose weight, quit smoking, become healthy, change jobs, get better grades, be more outgoing, make more money, get more done, start a new business, improve your relationships with certain persons, or whatever else, and if you really want to accomplish such goals, then by all means ask yourself if your goals meet the seven criteria. And, if they don't, take the time to modify or fix whatever you need to so that they do.

In discussing goals with several individuals at a seminar last year, a woman commented that her only goal for that particular week was to just get to 5:00 p.m. Friday. She said this in jest and we had a good laugh, but in truth many individuals live their lives exactly in this manner. They go from one week to the next never really zeroing in on their goals, never really finding the time to write them down, never really finding the time to develop a plan to achieve them, yet the *power* of having goals, truly having them, is enormous.

Goal power can be illustrated by the study done on the Princeton University 1953 graduating class. It was determined at graduation that only three percent of the graduating class had written goals. Twenty years later it was determined that those three percent who had goals had amassed more wealth than the entire remaining ninety-seven percent of the class!

Goals are important in all aspects of our lives—not just for pulling us toward financial gain (which may not even be one of your goals). Muhammad Ali, perhaps the greatest world heavyweight boxing champion of all times, said: *What keeps me going is goals.* And singer Linda Ronstadt said: *What you have to do is erect a fence and say, OK, scale this.*

Despite the existence of many examples like the above, most individuals still have difficulty truly grasping the essential nature of goals. Living life without goals is playing pin the tail on the donkey; living life *with* goals is removing the blindfold and then playing.

In Sum . . .

♦ Your goal choices are the interim milestones on your journey of life that will serve as magnets to provide the *power* necessary to pull you toward what you want to achieve.

♦ The most important thing about goals is that you have them.

♦ Those who set goals accomplish infinitely more than those who lack goals.

Menu Choices

In addition to epitaph and goal choices, you have many other choices before you in life. These are contained on countless menus from which you make daily selections.

Upon awakening each morning, one of the menus you can select from is the one that contains the expressions you will choose to show to others throughout the day. On one side of this menu are happy faces and on the other side are grumpy ones. Your choice. When you get to the office, to school, or wherever else you may be going, you can greet people with either a happy face and your smile, or a frown. Your choice. When you get home at night, the same menu of choices awaits you at the door. You can smile and say, "What a great day, God," or you can frown and say, "Great God, what a day." Take your pick, the choice is yours. As Napoleon Hill said, *It is always your next move.*

Just as you can choose to smile or scowl, you can choose to walk up the steps or ride the elevator, to drink or to drive, to have a can-do or a can't-do attitude, and so on.

Life each day is one menu after another, and you are there placing the orders. The items you select for today, tomorrow, and next week will build upon one another to form a pattern, and that pattern at your life's end will be who you have become.

Most individuals don't give a lot of thought to the fact that every choice on the menus of their lives is their own choice to make. It is all too easy to slip into the trap of rationalizing that someone else has caused or influenced us to make the choices. The reality, however, is that every choice, from the very big to the very small, is ours alone to make.

> *You always do whatever you want to do. This is true of every act. You may say you had to do something, or that you were forced to, but actually, whatever you do, you do by choice. Only you have the power to choose for yourself. The choice is yours. You hold the tiller. You can alter the course you choose in the direction of where you want to be—today, tomorrow, or in a distant time to come.*
> —W. Clement Stone

With choice, you hold the tiller, but keep in mind that you also hold the throttle, for choices, even if they are just menu choices, create the power.

.

In Sum . . .

◆ Menu choices are the selections you make throughout each day—these are conscious choices you alone can make.

◆ You can choose to be happy or sad, positive or negative—it is always your choice—but why choose sad if you can choose happy?

Choose Big For Big Power

Men are often capable of greater things than they perform. They are sent into the world with bills of credit and seldom draw to their full limit.

—Horace Walpole

One of the most exciting prospects in life is the infinite capacity of your personal power. You are a miracle, but you unleash miraculous powers only when you choose big. When you want something big, then you will see your real power. If you choose only modest goals, then you will never know what you are capable of.

Johann Wolfgang Von Goethe put it this way: *Dream no small dreams for they have no power to move the hearts of men.*

I have observed the effect of the big dreaming phenomenon over and over again—it is only the big challenges, the big dreams, that stir us.

Years ago when I was in the Jaycees, our particular chapter was having difficulty signing up new members and getting existing members involved. I saw all of these problems literally disappear overnight when we had the idea to purchase a mobile intensive care unit for our community. To raise the funds to get this done offered a large enough challenge to inspire us on. In three months, the money was raised, our membership roster was full, and we were all very involved. This example shows how raising our sights increases our enthusiasm for them.

Claude Bristol, the author of *The Magic of Believing,* wrote: *You have to think big to be big.* Dr. David J. Schwartz, the author of *The Magic of Thinking Big,* wrote: *How you think determines how you act. How you act in turn determines how others react to you.* The moral here is that if you think big and act big, others will respond in kind—they will think big and act big as well, and they will think big of you.

Each of us has an inexplicable super power hidden within that we can call upon to rise to an occasion. Unfortunately, if there is no occasion to rise to, we never call upon the power.

The power you summon from within is always in

proportion to the dimensions of your choices. So always choose BIG.

In Sum . . .

♦ Each of us has an inexplicable super power hidden within and it is released when we choose to accomplish big things with our lives.

Choosing Success Means Choosing Your Sacrifices

One aspect of choosing and getting what you want out of life is what Arnold Schwarzenegger referred to when he said, *No pain, no gain.* Sophocles put it this way: *There is no success without hardship.*

Every choice for success involves a two-fold sacrifice. First, by choosing one thing, you are not choosing another; you therefore are giving up a choice for something else. Second, every choice requires the pain and the hardship of making an effort to get what you have chosen.

Unless you try to do something beyond what you have mastered, you will never grow.
　　　　　　　　　　　　　　　—C.R. Lawton

There will always be a sacrifice required for results. It is the early bird who gives up sleeping in to get the worm. To get what you want, right on the heels of deciding what that is, you must also decide what you will do in exchange for the results you desire.

Will you give up desserts and sleeping in (so you can go for a morning walk) to get the body you want? Will you take some self-study courses in the evenings to advance your credentials? Will you give up television so you can write a book? What rewards do you want, and what will you forego to get them?

In Sum . . .

♦ There is no success without hardship, there is no gain without pain.

The Choice Of Time
And Your Tomorrows

The person who coined the phrase "time is money" has done a great injustice to the millions of individuals who accept this maxim as true. Time and money aren't even close to being comparable. *Time isn't money. Time is life itself.*

When you spend your time, you spend your life. Because of this, some of your most significant choices are the ones you make about *how you spend your time*.

That isn't sand sifting through the hourglass— it's your life. When the sand runs out, you don't get another turn. Arthur Lipper III, the former publisher of *Venture* magazine, put this into perspective when he wrote: *No one dies wishing they had spent more time with their business.*

Time is not just our most precious resource. In actuality, time is our only true resource. As Ernest Hemingway put it, *Time is all we have.* We tend to disregard time until we have used it all up, yet at life's end, we won't be able to buy back a single hour, let alone a day, week, or year. The point is, we can now! That is the power of choice. Right now, you can buy all of your tomorrows just by choosing them! As Marcus Aurelius wrote: *Do not live as though you had a thousand years before you.*

Choosing your tomorrows is an awesome and exciting phenomenon when you think about it. When you exercise the choices you have over how to spend your time tomorrow, you are deciding more than what happens as the sand seeps through the hourglass. You are buying your future. Since big tomorrows cost the same as little tomorrows, buy BIG.

> *Tomorrow is the most important thing in life. Comes into us at midnight very clear. It's perfect when it arrives and it puts itself in our hands. It hopes we've learned something from yesterday.*
>
> —John Wayne

As Leigh Mitchell Hodge put it: *Life begins each morning!* The clay of your tomorrow will arrive in your hands at midnight. You get to decide what to make of it. You get to choose, and when you do, you are choosing yourself!

In Sum . . .

◆ Tomorrow is the most important thing in life. It arrives perfectly at midnight; choose to make it special.

And What If You Don't Know What You Want?

A real frustration for many individuals is that they don't know what they want to *be,* they don't know what they want to *do,* and they don't know how to go about finding out—that is, they can't choose because they don't know what options they have. Some individuals are further frustrated because they think they are limiting their choices in life by making a choice.

An answer to this dilemma and to these frustrations is to fire a shot into the bushes and see what kinds of birds fly out. By this I mean you have to move out into life and see what's there. You have to get wet to learn how to swim.

The problem for some individuals is that they see life as a river with them in the middle of it looking upstream as choices come their way. Life to these people is a matter of waiting for the right choice to come along.

Unfortunately, life is not a river—it is an ocean. We have to swim out into it, and often we have to begin swimming before we can see the horizon.

Several years ago I had lunch with a friend who was really frustrated with his present position but he didn't know exactly what he could do to alter his present circumstances. I asked him what he thought he might like to do instead of what he was doing. He didn't know. So, I suggested he join a civic group to start meeting some new people and that he come with me to a venture capital luncheon for entrepreneurs. Within a year he started his own business—what he needed was a fresh perspective—he had to get in motion to get it.

If you don't know what you want in life, then it's up to you to start getting some input so that your mind can begin to evaluate the alternatives. When my daughter selected a college, we requested dozens of brochures and then visited several schools so she could decide. If you don't know what you want to do, get some fresh input. Read some books. Visit some new locations. Talk to some new people. Take a course. Take a trip. Go to the library. Get something for your mind to digest so it can spit out an answer.

When I took Lewis Timberlake's advice in 1983 and wrote my epitaph, I realized I was on the wrong road, but I didn't know then which road I might ultimately want to be on. The truth is, I've rewritten my epitaph a couple of times since 1983, and the career part I want to be remembered for is still evolving. But the important part is this: I'm in motion, moving toward what I want to be moving toward—by my *choice*.

In Sum . . .

♦ Oftentimes individuals don't know exactly what they want in life, so they do nothing but wait for choices to come their way.

♦ But life is not a river with choices flowing our way—it is an ocean, and we must begin swimming toward a horizon.

———————

You need only choose . . . That is all you need to do. Then . . . everything is yours . . .
                                        —Vernon Howard

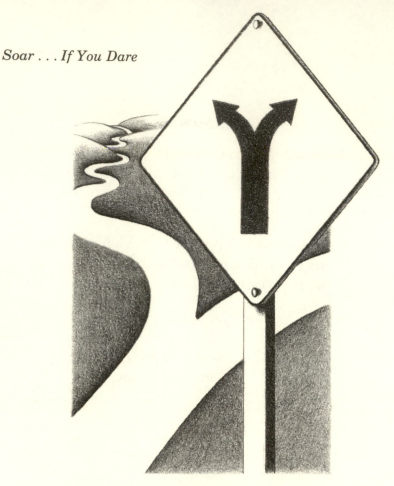

The Power of Your Choices
What To Do. . .

1. Resolve to take responsibility for yourself by pro-actively making the choices in your life.

2. Set aside some uninterrupted time daily to think through and make your choices and goal selections.

3. Always be able to tell others what you are and what you are becoming.

4. Write out your epitaph consisting of a single sentence you want those important to you to be able to read about each component of your life.

5. Always have at least three written goals you want to accomplish: today; tomorrow; next week; next month; next year.

6. Make positive choices in all situations.

7. Make no little choices, for little choices create little power; instead, choose BIG for big power—choose greatness.

8. Decide what you will give in return for what you want in life, make the commitment to give it, and begin the deed.

9. Spend a few minutes each evening planning and visualizing your tomorrows. Jot down your plans, commit to them, and upon rising, begin living them immediately.

10. Don't get frozen in place because you haven't yet made choices as to what you want in life. Resolve to get in motion to expand your horizons so you know about more choices.

11. Read, travel, meet with people, become informed, get exposure—by all means seek life out. DO NOT wait for it to come to you.

The key to your universe is that you have choice.

—Carl Frederick

Five

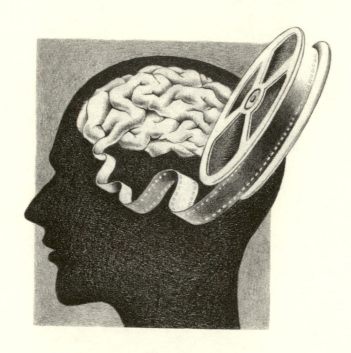

Your imagination has the power to create a mental picture of your future in your mind that then will become the reality of your life.

The Power Of Your Imagination

MANY PEOPLE have difficulty fathoming and accepting that they literally can use their imaginations to create their futures.

This is understandable. Using our imaginations in this way is akin to magic or supernatural phenomena, like having the ability to work miracles, which is not the kind of thing people readily acknowledge they believe in.

Ralph Waldo Emerson wrote: *There is nothing capricious in nature, and the implanting of desire indicates that its gratification is in the constitution of the creature that feels it.* Richard Bach told us that we are never given a wish without also being given the power to make it true.

There is abundant evidence that it is the imaginative powers of individuals that have brought about every advancement we enjoy today. Everything human beings have created, they first created as a dream. Mike Vance, who worked with Walt Disney in conceiving and creating Disney World, relates that when someone commented to him how sad it was that Walt Disney did not live to see his dream of Disney World completed, Vance smiled and replied that Walt Disney *did* see Disney World completed, *in his dreams*. And that is why we have Disney World today, only because he did dream it, see it, and make it happen.

We all have the ability to use our imaginations to solve problems and to help us achieve our goals. But it is easy to get so wrapped up in the pace of our daily activity traps that we forget to take time to relax, sit back, dream a little, and allow our imaginations to begin the work they were intended for—to create visions of what our futures could be like and will be like so that is what they become.

Our imaginations are a tool to be put to use, but as with any tool, the process of using it is a skill that will take some practice to develop. Just as you learned to use a pencil, a shovel, or a computer, with effort you can learn to use your imagination to bring about the future you have in mind.

In Sum . . .

♦ Everything humans created, they first created as a dream.

♦ Your imagination is a power that you can use to create your future, but you must learn the techniques and skills to use your imagination to your advantage.

Images Held In Your Mind Will Come True!

The phenomenon whereby we become what we think about all day long is not a new concept, but the importance of this does seem to get discounted or lost in the shuffle. I know very few individuals who truly are consciously aware of what they think about, and I know fewer still who set aside some time and pro-actively plan and manage their own thinking habits.

This is puzzling when you consider how many hundreds of wise men and women have written about the process whereby the thoughts in our minds become our realities.

Dr. Norman Vincent Peale wrote of this concept in *The Power of Positive Thinking,* and he expanded upon it in *Positive Imagining;* Dr. David Schwartz entitled his book on the subject *The Magic of Thinking*

Big; Claude M. Bristol wrote *The Magic of Believing;* Dr. Robert Schuller referred to it frequently in *Possibility Thinking;* and Napoleon Hill wrote that we can literally *Think and Grow Rich.*

You can read a hundred self-help or motivational books and you invariably will find some reference to the same underlying message. I know, because I have read them and the message is there repeatedly: *The mental images you hold in your mind will come true.*

Take a moment and ponder the meaning of this, and let me repeat it because it is so important: *The images you hold in your mind will come true.* This does not mean that the images you hold in your mind *may* come true—it means they *will* come true.

In other words, your imagination not only *foretells* your future, *it causes it!* And this works just as well for the big opportunities in life as it does for the little ones. When you see yourself making a good first impression, you make one. When you imagine finishing the assignment on time, you do. When you visualize a promotion and actually imagine it being given to you, you get it.

In Sum . . .

♦ The images you hold in your mind will come true! Your imagination will cause your future.

The Power Of Our Subconscious Minds

While the images we hold in our minds will be transformed into our realities, the flip side is that those images *not* in our minds can't possibly become our realities. In other words, goals will not be achieved until they are first specified within the imagination.

It is important to recognize that images in our minds will become realities even if those images are negative or undesirable in any way. Our imaginative powers are not selective—we tend to implement whatever we imagine, in the manner and form that we imagine it. As Dr. Peale said: *We tend to get what we expect*.

On the other hand, although everything begins with thought, it does not follow that *all* of our thoughts will become a reality. Life is not that way; there are some disappointments for each of us. However, thoughts that tend to become realities are those that we think about often and that are complete to the point that they can be acted upon. What many individuals who want to use the power of their imagination fail to understand is just how vivid and complete their imaged thoughts must be.

For example, to think *I want to be successful* is meaningless because "successful" is a generality, and our subconscious minds can't relate to it or act upon it. If we were to go a step further and define success as flying to the moon or selling a million records, even that is meaningless to many individuals because they can't relate to or understand what it means to be an astronaut or a recording artist.

> *You are searching for the magic key that will unlock the door to the source of power; and yet you have the key in your hands, and you may use it the moment you learn to control your thoughts.*
>
> —Napoleon Hill

Our subconscious minds are our implementing minds, our auto pilots that guide us to our goals. Our subconscious minds cannot and will not begin to move us toward our goals, however, until they first can visualize what it will be like when those goals are obtained. In our examples, we have to be able to visualize what is it like to orbit the Earth or cut a tape.

That is the key—*visualizing what it will be like.* In order to do that, our thinking must be complete—in other words, if we don't know what it is like to blast off in a rocket, then we have to do some homework and find out so we can visualize achieving the goal in specific parameters. The same principle applies to all goals for success, regardless of what they are. If your long-term success goal is to become a superlative teacher, then you can't begin to move toward being "superlative" until you start to define superlative in your mind in concrete terms that your subconscious mind can actually "see."

Remember, however, that your subconscious mind implements *all* that you imagine—not just your long-term goals. A teacher who imagines winning over a difficult student will do so, but a mail carrier who holds an image of a dog attacking will be forever wary of dogs. We tend to fulfill our expectations, whatever they are.

> *Your subconscious mind never wanders; it always pays attention. It is always ready to make happen in your life those things—positive and negative—that you are imagining.*
> —Leland Cooley

The powers of imagination are not hocus-pocus powers existing only in fairy tales. They are very real forces in the universe, and they are used in everyday life, sometimes for very big achievements.

In the 1960s, our space program was intact, but nothing special. Then President Kennedy solidified NASA's efforts by implanting an image of success in everyone's mind: *We are going to put a man on the moon by the end of the decade.* These simple words defined a vision everyone at NASA could literally see in their minds. That is, they could *imagine* it. That done, the physical reality could take place as well, and it did.

Where there is no vision, the people perish.
—Proverbs:29:18

Another example of imaging techniques made headlines during the 1991 baseball season when the Atlanta Braves hired Jack Llewellyn, a psychologist and recognized expert in the mental imagery field, to work with Braves' pitcher John Smoltz. Smoltz's pitching record went from 2-11 in the first half of the season to 12-2 in the second half, and Llewellyn was considered the dividing line. Llewellyn created a video tape of Smoltz's best pitches and had Smoltz view the video over and over. When he wasn't viewing the video, Smoltz was instructed to visualize the video in his mind, to *imagine* himself pitching perfect pitches. The Braves didn't win the World Series, but Smoltz's pitching performance was considered stellar—the best in his career! The mental imagery worked.

The whole idea . . . is to enable you to mentally see the picture at all times of the day.
—Claude M. Bristol

In January 1986 I read an article in *Piedmont Airlines* magazine entitled *Telling Your Own Fortune,* which pointed out that the future is not as obscure as most people imagine it. *To a degree, it is possible for all of us to take a reliable look at tomorrow and determine how things might turn out,* the article said. But it went on, *we must remember that we live in a cause and effect world . . . Be not deceived. What you sow, that you will reap. Sow the wrong seeds and you will reap the wrong harvest. Sow the right seeds and you can expect the right harvest.*

This was not intended as an ominous admonition, but as a reminder of the *marvelous promise* of cause and effect in our lives—that is, we can create the effects we want by altering the causes, which are our actions and our thoughts.

A particular story I liked in the magazine article is a reminder of "fishing," a carnival game I played many times as a kid by paying a dime to a man who held forth a bundle of strings, each of which went up in the air, through a hoop, then down to a prize on one of the shelves. This is an example of cause and effect because I determined my prize by reaching out, selecting a string, and pulling it to see what prize I had won. Cause and effect.

"Be careful," the author wrote, "about the strings you pull in life. You always get what is on the other side."

You always get what is on the other side—this is true also of the strings you imagine pulling in your mind.

A common mistake is to *limit* the expectations of our imaginations, or to narrow the areas of our lives

where we think the powers of our imaginations can
be put to good use.

> *The starting point of all achievement is
> desire. Keep this constantly in mind. Weak
> desire brings weak results, just as a small
> amount of fire makes a small amount of heat.*
> —Napoleon Hill

There are no limits to where and how we can use
the powers of our imaginations. We can use them to
advance our careers, to get better grades, to achieve
goals, to lose weight, and even to make us well such
as in these examples:

> In *Reversing Heart Disease,* Dr. Julian M.
> Whitaker wrote: "You need a beautiful men-
> tal picture of a healthy heart, lungs, arter-
> ies, and blood doing their work the way they
> are meant to. Keeping that positive image
> in your mind will encourage you to improve
> your health."

> *The Journal of Orthopaedic Sports Therapy*
> reported that women who visualized isomet-
> ric exercises for 20 minutes strengthened
> their thigh muscles 12.6% in just four days.

> In the March 1992 issue of *Reader's Digest*
> an article entitled *Think Yourself Thin*
> featured a condensation of *The Wellness*

Book written by individuals at the Mind/Body Institute. The message of the article? *If you're trying to lose weight, don't overlook a powerful diet tool: your mind.*

In Sum . . .

♦ The images in our minds, positive or negative, will become our realities.

♦ Thoughts created in our conscious minds will be transferred to and implemented by our subconscious minds through repeated vivid and specific visualizations.

♦ Visualize your successes, then you can achieve them.

♦ Life is a constant cause and effect phenomenon and what you think (cause) will result in your realities (effect). You therefore can create your future by choosing and developing your thoughts.

Your Personal Crystal Ball Is A Crystal Wall

Have you ever seen one of those black crystal ball toys that work by asking a question and then turning the ball upside down to see the answer? These crystal balls provide no answers unless you make the effort to turn them upside down and look. The act of looking actually causes the future to occur, so to speak. This concept is fascinating because it is exactly the way our personal crystal balls work, except that they are not balls, they are *crystal walls.*

Our crystal walls are the miles and miles of translucent walls separating our conscious minds from our mysterious subconscious minds. These crystal walls are sky high and impenetrable; we can't get over them or through them and there are no doorways. But that's okay—these crystal walls are actually a magic movie screen for use in transferring sight and sound from our conscious minds to our subconscious minds.

When you create images on the conscious side of your mind, you play a mental video tape on your crystal walls. Because the surfaces of the walls are translucent, the video images and soundtrack are played on the subconscious side of your mind. Once this happens, your subconscious mind can see the objective; and when your subconscious mind can see the objective, it can move toward it. Without the mental video image displayed on your crystal walls, there is nothing to implement because all that your subconscious mind sees is a blank screen.

> *Nothing happens unless first a dream.*
> —Carl Sandburg

Your crystal walls are reliable as a foreteller of

the future, but they also are extremely powerful in *bringing about* the future. You become what you think about because it is impossible to do otherwise.

Individuals are successful because they imagine themselves as achieving only success and they therefore can't be anything but successful.

To fail we usually have to first imagine it. The students who say, oh I'll probably get a C or D, probably do. The job applicants who imagine that they're not hiring today, don't get hired.

Whatever you're imagining, you have a team ten thousand strong on the subconscious side of your mind with "implementation" on their jerseys. They are ready, willing, and able to accomplish whatever you want, but first you must call them to action.

How do you call your team into action? How do you tell them the plays? How do you motivate them to get going on your behalf?

The only way you can communicate with your team is through your crystal walls—by showing your team a mental video. This is the art of crystal walling.

> *We do not yet trust the unknown powers of thought. Whence came all these tools, inventions, books, laws, . . . kingdoms? Out of the invisible world, through a few brains. The arts and institutions of men are created out of thought.*
>
> —Ralph Waldo Emerson

It is useful to think of implementing the crystal walling technique as the acquisition of two *habits*. The first is the habit of holding mental images of what you *do* want to happen, and the second is the habit of eliminating mental images of what you *don't* want to happen. For a few fortunate individuals this comes naturally, but for most of us it takes time and effort before it becomes routine. Don't let this discourage you, however, because the lifetime benefits of this technique are tremendous.

Until crystal walling becomes ingrained in your daily life, it may be helpful to think of your mental images as a collection of personal video tapes that you select and play periodically throughout each day. For example, take a few minutes right now, relax in a comfortable chair, and imagine clicking into your mental VCR a personal video of what you want your tomorrow morning to be like. Close your eyes and watch the video play on the conscious side of your mind. See yourself get up. Note the time. Then see what you do next. Work through the various mental images of getting up tomorrow, taking a shower, selecting the exact clothes you will wear, eating breakfast, and so on. See everything in detail—the greater the detail, the better. Make everything in color. Hear your voice. Listen to what you are saying.

When you take the time to *consciously* create and work through images like those, you are creating

126

moving pictures in your mind at the speed of light and in just a few moments you can create the essence of a video of the way you want tomorrow morning to be. Although you are not aware of it, your subconscious mind is observing this video as you create it on the conscious side of your mind. As a result, when you get up in the morning, your subconscious mind now knows the game plan and that is what you will get.

> *It is a psychological law that whatever we wish to accomplish, we must impress upon the subconscious mind.*
> —Orison Swett Marden

Sometimes, events will occur to alter some of the tomorrow mornings you plan, but those will be the exceptions; most times, it will work out very close to the video you create on your crystal walls.

Visualizing images of tomorrow morning is a simple exercise, but the principles involved are exactly the same for planning your tomorrow morning a year from now. That means you can predict your future and bring it about by creating and running a video on your crystal walls today!

An interesting exercise is to ask yourself what your personal film footage from the *Lifestyles of the Rich and Famous* will look like for your life ten years from now. What will be in that video? How will you look? Where will you be living? What kind of car will you be driving? What model? What color?

It likely will not surprise you to learn that most individuals can't bring to mind a video like I just described, and the reason is simple: They haven't yet taken the time to create it.

When you are able to answer the kinds of questions like those raised above for your *lifestyle* video ten years from now (or even for a year from now), you have *begun* the process of determining your future.

The power of your imagination gives you the miracle opportunity to script and direct your future from the ground up without limitations—you can produce your tomorrow by creating it today—in a video in your mind, to be played over and over again on your magic crystal walls—so that it will then become your reality.

An important point is that thoughts precede reality, not vice versa. The images in your mind don't get there because of reality; rather, it is reality that comes about because of the images.

To use your power of imagination for achieving success, first you must create your personal library of mental videos containing the images you desire— like a selection of career videos to foretell the future of your career, or a selection of personal appearance videos to show you what you are going to look like, and so on. Then, you must get into the *daily habit* of playing the videos on your crystal walls. These are substantial tasks, but the return on the time invested in them will be nothing short of remarkable.

A personal example I can provide is when my partner and I started our own business in 1984. We needed to raise money, so we rehearsed what we would say when asking people to invest in our endeavors. Then I went off by myself and imagined the specific people I would talk to. I envisioned them raising all kinds of possible objections, but I also imagined what I would say and what I would do in response. As a result, we raised the funds we desired in just a few months—just like we expected to—just like I imagined it happening.

The results in my example are not the exception to the rule. People do get what they imagine. You can apply this power to any of your goals, and that is precisely what you should do to achieve success.

Your daily video habit will be reinforced by any physical reminders you can devise. Perhaps you might clip a picture of a car or house you want to own or the physique you want to have and post it on a bulletin board. You might prepare a chart illustrating your goals or design a mock business card with your new title on it. Physical reminders are props to your mental videos; in addition to triggering the playing of your videos themselves, props will make your videos more real.

An American figure skater had trouble getting up every morning at 5:00 to train . . . until she placed a photo of the Russian champion by her alarm. Under the picture were the words: "Comrade, while you were sleeping, I was training."

—Ron Gilbert

Like any other self-improvement program, crystal walling requires a reasonable investment of time over the long haul. The creation and holding of mental pictures is not a quick fix, a fad diet, or an instant formula for success—forget about trying this for just a few days or even for a few weeks. To get results, make a commitment to spend a little time exercising your imagination *each and every day for the rest of your life.*

In Sum . . .

♦ Our subconscious minds are our implementing minds, and we must program them with what we want implemented— like a blank screen, our subconscious minds await our instructions.

♦ A reason many individuals don't use the power of their imaginations to create their futures is that they don't have a readily available supply of mental videos to play in their minds for use in creating and bringing about their futures.

◆ The literal creative powers of our imaginations are just as real as any power in nature, yet few people appreciate this phenomenon and fewer still take the *time* and *effort* to apply it to real world situations—those that do, get results, those that don't, don't.

Shattering Self-Limiting Images

In addition to creating and playing the *positive* images you desire, it is equally important to *eliminate* from your thoughts images of results you don't desire or don't want to happen.

Undesirable images must be cast out! One technique is to imagine shattering the crystal wall upon which the negative image is playing. Just imagine physically shattering the unwanted image. Do this immediately any time you have the negative thought. Another technique is to imagine reaching into your mind with a magic hand and lifting out the undesirable thought or image. These ideas may seem a little nonsensical, but I have used both techniques with excellent results.

Remember that all self-limiting images are *learned* images. You weren't born with any of the self-limiting images that you possibly have now—this may seem extraordinary, but it's true. All self-limiting images, be they *limiting* images of capabilities, desire, deservedness, or self-esteem—all of these undesirable images were *taught* to you by someone (maybe even yourself) and you learned them.

The good news is that anything learned can be unlearned, and this is done by creating new images in place of the old ones.

You were born with only two natural fears, the fear of loud noises and the fear of falling. This means that the fear of failure had to be learned; this being the case, it can be unlearned, regardless of what you are afraid of failing at—be it your career, your family life, your social life, or any other aspect of your life.

> *Our destiny changes with our thought; we shall become what we wish to become, do what we wish to do, when our habitual thought corresponds with our desire.*
> —Orison Swett Marden

One of the big reasons individuals do not get what they want in life is they are in the habit of holding images that are contrary to their stated goals. Your images must be consistent with the goals you wish to achieve. You can alter the images you hold by choosing to do so and by replacing undesirable images with positive images of what you want to believe or what you want to become.

If you see yourself in your mind as someone who just keeps plugging along, then that is what you will be. Shatter that image and replace it with a mental video of you accomplishing something you will be proud of—something you will be happy to have others read on your epitaph. Then go for it.

In Sum . . .

◆ All self-limiting images were learned and if they could be learned, they can be unlearned.

◆ The images you hold must be consistent with your desired goals.

Five minutes, just before you go to sleep, given to a bit of directed imagination regarding achievement possibilities of the morrow, will steadily and increasingly bear fruit, particularly if all ideas of difficulty, worry or fear are resolutely ruled out and replaced by those of accomplishment and smiling courage.

—Frederick Pierce

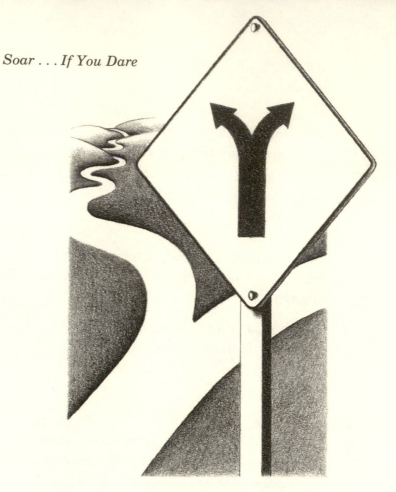

The Power Of Your Imagination
What To Do . . .

1. Resolve to learn, apply, and practice the techniques
   necessary to utilize your power of imagination
   until those techniques become skills of habit.

2. Become consciously aware of the mental images
   you hold in your mind, for they will come true.

3. Begin to become aware of the images you do *not*
   have in your mind (but which you desire), as you

must create these in your mind so they can become the realities of your tomorrows.

4. Develop your own collection of mental videos depicting your achievements of what you want in life. Make these detailed and real and create a separate video for each major aspect of your life—it may be useful to think of your roles as the writer, the director, and the producer.

5. Prepare an inventory of your videos and periodically review the inventory to make sure your mental videos are up-to-date and consistent with your goals and objectives.

6. Get into the *daily and life-long habit* of continuously holding mental images of what you want to happen. Think of this as playing desired videos in your mental VCR and consciously see those videos on the crystal walls of your mind. Play your mental videos particularly at bedtime.

7. Get into the *daily and life-long habit* of continuously eliminating from your mind images of things you don't want to happen—including the elimination or shattering of any images that are limitation images.

8. Make sure you are playing each of your videos periodically. It does no good to just create the video images of what you want to happen—you must play them repeatedly.

*Picture yourself in
your mind's eye as
having already
achieved this goal.
See yourself doing
the things you'll be
doing when you've
reached your goal.*

—Earl Nightingale

Six

The most obvious of all requirements for success, however you define success, is this: To achieve your goals in life, you must act.

The Power Of Your Actions

A MAN prayed hard to win the lottery for a week and yet he did not win. So, he repeated this prayer in earnest ten times a day for three weeks: "Dear God, please let me win the lottery, I really need to win."

When he still did not win, he dropped to his knees and wailed his disappointment to God: "Why have you forsaken me?"

God replied in thunder from the Heavens: "Give me a break! Buy a ticket!"

Life is that way. You have to buy a ticket to get results, and buying a ticket means taking actions toward your goals. As Og Mandino wrote on the Scroll marked IX in *The Greatest Salesman In The World: My dreams are worthless, my plans are dust, my goals are impossible. All are of no value unless they are followed by action. I will act now.*

Acting *now* means working toward your goals now, and, if you have big goals, it means putting forth big actions *now* by working hard *now* for long hours over sustained periods.

The power of action is often overlooked or ignored, and it is all too easy to forget that goals without actions will always just remain wishes. Moreover, many individuals do not understand that our actions create our power—not the power of our actions themselves, but a greater power called momentum. When we take an action, we get things going.

> *God gives every bird its food, but he does not throw it into the nest.*
> —J.G. Holland

There's a story about Hank Aaron during the 1957 World Series, when Yogi Berra, the Yankee catcher, noticed how Aaron grasped the bat and said: "Turn it around, so you can see the trademark." But Aaron ignored Berra and kept his eye on the pitcher's mound and said: "Didn't come up here to read. Came up here to hit." That is what we all have to do if we want to achieve success. We have to take action. We have to hit.

In Sum . . .

♦ The most obvious of all laws for success is this: You must take action to get results.

Don't Be An I Wisher In Life— Get In Motion

The world is filled with millions and millions of "I wishers," individuals who wish for much, but who will never see their wishes come true because they aren't also doers. Surely you have heard someone make a remark like, "Boy, I wish I could play the piano like that." Or, "I sure wish I had a swimming pool in my backyard." Or perhaps, "I really wish I had a great job like hers."

Truth is, the I wishers could have what they are wishing for—if they would only quit wishing and start putting forth the effort to get it! Many people say they'd like to play the piano, but most successful pianists act on it their entire lifetime.

An example of this is when a woman dashed up to the famous violinist Fritz Kreisler and bubbled, "I'd give my whole life to play as beautifully as you do." Said Kreisler: "I did."

Choosing what you want in life and imaging the

attainment of those goals are required steps for success, but they are not enough! If that is all you do, you will not be successful. Arnold Schwarzenegger didn't get his Mr. Universe body overnight—he spent years and years developing it. Thomas Edison didn't just wish for the light bulb, he took the actions of ten thousand experiments to invent it. (10,000!)

> *Parties who want milk should not seat themselves on a stool in the middle of a field in hope that the cow will back up to them.*
> —Elbert Hubbard

When Norman Vincent Peale wrote *The Power Of Positive Thinking,* he did not write that positive thinking alone would bring about results desired. When W. Clement Stone coined the phrase *"Positive Mental Attitude"* he did not proclaim that that alone would lead to success. And when Napoleon Hill wrote in *Think and Grow Rich* that *whatever the mind of man can conceive, man can achieve,* he did not then go on to say that achievements would occur without work. In fact, Hill went on to say that *hard work . . . through the transformation of definite plans* is required.

There are no quick fixes in life. You are not going to find them in this book or any other. There are no easy roads to success. There is no escaping the reality that hard work and determination are requisites for the achievement of results. You must be prepared to act, and you must be prepared to make sacrifices. Then you must act and make the sacrifices.

In each thousand-mile journey, you must take that first step. Then you must take the second step, the third, the fourth, and all the other steps required for all the journeys toward all the goals that you have in your life. If you want water, don't toss a coin in the well and wish for water—drop in the bucket instead and hoist it up.

Action is life, or, to put it bluntly, without action there is not life, but death. When action stops, life stops—there is no such thing as *still life,* there is only still death.

> *Life is action, the use of one's powers. And to use them to their height is our joy and duty . . .*
> — Unknown

Don't get caught in life waiting for someone to buy you a ticket. They're all too busy buying their own ticket to remember yours. You must take responsibility for yourself, and that means getting in gear. You alone can move the gearshift from park to drive. You alone can put the pedal to the metal and turn the wheel.

If you want a new job, you must be the one to find it. If you want better grades, you have to be the one to study. If you want to change your home, your environment, or anything else in your life, then you must be the one to act.

Action precedes and leads to all progress. Action will bring results. Choose to live your life to the fullest by choosing to act. Then act to your fullest. As Elbert Hubbard wrote: *Do your work with your whole heart and you will succeed—there's so little competition.*

In Sum . . .

♦ The "I Wishers" in life will not see their wishes come true unless they pursue their wishes with commitment, hard work, determination and a willingness to make sacrifices.

♦ You must act, and now is the time.

The Magic Of Beginning

Beginning usually will be the hardest part about any task you set before yourself. If you are going to get stuck, more than at any other point you will get stuck at the beginning.

People tend to underestimate the effort required of beginning. This in itself is a problem because they suddenly are overwhelmed, and this grinds them to another halt. This happens because individuals don't have a specific beginning clearly in mind. They want to begin a journey of a thousand miles, but they

146

haven't yet truly imagined taking that specific first step. A journey like this will never be taken.

Well begun is half done.
> — Aristotle

Isaac Newton's laws of physics apply to people the same way they apply to other elements in nature. It should be no surprise that we have a natural tendency to procrastinate because procrastination is just one form of inertia; a body at rest tends to remain at rest.

For this reason, far more people fail before the starting lines in life than they do after them. This does not have to be the case, however. Procrastination is just one of many obstacles that will have to be conquered. It can be overcome, but this requires effort and determination. It also requires commitment.

A problem here is that our minds have difficulty in interpreting commitment and determination because they are elusive and intangible. While that doesn't mean it is impossible to get determination and commitment, it does mean that we have to transform the intangible into the tangible, which involves a physical change of some kind.

Depending on the circumstances, I have found it helpful to make a commitment to myself about a *specific* future time when I will begin major tasks. This procedure has the advantage of conserving physical energy until it is needed while mobilizing my thinking immediately. Like having my cake and eating it too, I get to put beginning off a bit; meanwhile, my mind is already hard at work. Fixating on beginning at a specific moment in time concentrates thinking and physical energies on that single moment, thus providing the extra bit of energy when it is needed to overcome inertia at the beginning. I don't always set some future date to begin because this loses the advantage of beginning immediately. Beginning something new right away has the advantage of birth enthusiasm brought about by the newness of the idea or task. This immediacy provides extra energy to get momentum going, which can be quite an advantage.

> *Winning starts with beginning.*
> —Robert H. Schuller

Beginning immediately, whatever the task is, can be a double-edged sword, however. One disadvantage of beginning anything immediately (that is, as soon as the idea or task is conceived) is that the beginning may not have been thought through sufficiently. This can result in a weak or false start, which in turn could be disastrous. Another disadvantage of beginning immediately is that this will preempt whatever else was on your agenda, thus breaking concentration on other high-priority projects.

A happy compromise sometimes is to begin

simply by writing down what it is you are going to do and when you are going to think it through more thoroughly. Writing down a plan to plan, so to speak.

In Sum . . .

♦ More people fail by not beginning than in any other way. Extra effort should be applied to all of your beginnings to ensure they get launched properly.

♦ There is a magical power in beginning, and once we are going, we tend to be able to keep on going.

Beginning By Writing It Down

I recommend that major goals be pursued by first writing down the essential tasks that must be accomplished for the goals to be achieved. This organizes the effort and it avoids omission of key items.

Perhaps the most important reason to begin by writing things down, however, is that to begin anything, what we must do first is activate the process of making tangible that which is intangible. We must commence the transformation of thought into physical reality. The easiest, most elegant way known to man to begin converting an intangible thought into a tangible reality is simply this: *Write it down.*

Writing anything down is a tangible, physical act that is a power that most people fail to recognize, understand, and utilize to its fullest advantage. The objective is to begin the transformation of thought to reality, and a pen moving across paper does just that.

> *All glory comes from daring to begin.*
> —Eugene F. Ware

If you are ever having difficulty beginning anything, begin by writing it down. "It" can be a list of key tasks, a complete plan, or just "to do" items. It can also be a sketch or some notations of ideas or thoughts. It can be on the back of an envelope or on a computer. What you write and where are not as important as the act itself. The objective is to get something down because this signifies that you have begun and it commences the build-up of momentum.

A side benefit of writing things down is that you are then provided the opportunity to evaluate and refine your own thinking, which is essential for two reasons. First, contrary to some popular perceptions, our initial judgments and interpretations are more often inferior or mediocre than superior. Judgment is like a good stew—it usually improves with age. (It also frequently improves with the age of the cook, not just the stew, but not always.) Second, our initial thinking on many important subjects is oftentimes more incomplete than complete. Most people spend too little time thinking; after all, thinking is hard—it is the hardest work that we all do.

Words you write to yourself are revelations of the thoughts within your being. Your written words are pictures of what you are thinking. The only way you can physically *see* your thoughts is to write them down or sketch them out. If your thinking is incomplete, this will be immediately obvious to you upon seeing them on paper. Your thoughts will then begin to develop and change instantly.

What is really interesting is that often we do not even know what we *think* that we think until we write it down. We can all *say* things we haven't thought about yet, but it's impossible to write things we haven't thought about.

In addition to writing it down, you might want to try tackling your beginnings (and middles and ends, for that matter) by bite-sizing them. That is, break down your beginnings into bite-sized chunks, such as tasks that can be done within an hour. If a beginning is any longer than this, it is going to be much easier to put it off. Who has a half-day to spare, right? But who can't fit in an hour?

An example of bite-sizing beginnings is how I approach my own writings, which is easy to put off. I deal with it by sitting down to write just a little, maybe for an hour, or just long enough to finish a small segment of a project. Invariably, I get lost in the writing about three minutes after I have begun and I end up writing for much longer than I had planned. I basically trick myself. It's a little game I play because it's good for me, and it works.

> *Once you are moving, you can keep moving.*
> —Ralph Alan Weill

Once we begin something, we tend to continue it. This tendency, in Isaac Newton's laws of physics, is also referred to as inertia—only this time it refers to the tendency of a body in motion to stay in that motion. (In physics, rest is only a special case of motion, so that inertia can refer to both.) Beginning works magic because it sets things in motion and then they tend to stay that way. By beginning we can all work magic!

A good exercise is to ask yourself what you really want in life and then to ask what you did yesterday, are doing today, and will do tomorrow to get it. Your answers may surprise you—you also may learn that you don't have ready answers to these questions.

In Sum . . .

♦ Writing things down is a power in itself. The simple act of putting pen to paper immediately collects and focuses our thoughts and brings us closer towards their realization.

◆ Thinking is hard work and we often do not even know our thoughts until we first write them down.

◆ If you ever have a problem, any problem, and don't know how to solve it, begin by putting something down on paper and new insights will flow to you instantly.

The Power Of Momentum Is Released By Having A Plan

There is another law in physics that we must address if we want to maximize the effectiveness of our actions toward our goals. We must exert power in all that we do. Power is required to overcome the obstacles we encounter. Power is required to build up and maintain momentum even in the face of resistance.

Imagine a giant cruise ship stationary at dock with its bow resting against the wharf. Even if the engines were turned on to maximum capacity in an effort to drive the ship into the wharf, the ship would likely stay right where it is and cause little or no damage.

But back that same ship up a mile and then have it cruise forward toward the wharf, even at only a few knots. Then stand back and watch. The full force of the ship applied to the bow will slice through the wharf. The difference in the two cases is momentum.

All great masters are chiefly distinguished by the power of adding a second, a third and perhaps a fourth step in a continuous line . . . with every step you enhance immensely the value of your first step.
                              —Ralph Waldo Emerson

The way we can create and maintain momentum in our lives is to have a plan full of goals and to persistently pursue them. Choosing what we want to achieve in life is a part of planning, but it is not all there is to planning. The creation of a plan also involves choosing the actions we will take and orchestrating the manner and order in which we intend to take them. This creates and maintains momentum for a simple reason: *We always know what to do immediately next.*

A life that hasn't a definite plan is likely to become driftwood.
                              —David Sarnoff

We run out of steam, and hence out of momentum, when we run out of meaningful tasks and projects to do and when we have to stop and think through what to do next. Such gaps in the flow of our actions cause breaks in our energy, and breaks in our energy bring us to a stop. When we stop, we must start again. This start, in turn, is another beginning, which requires extra energy, and we are back where we started.

People who maintain momentum in life get the most done simply because they use their energies and resources in the most effective ways possible.

The trick to maintaining momentum is al-ways having something to look forward to and always being able to look back at some-thing accomplished. Always be planning something. Always have written goals you are pursuing.

— Unknown

If you don't always know what to do next, you will hesitate, and a sufficient amount of hesitation will bring you to a standstill. The objective then is to minimize hesitation or eliminate it completely and the only way I know to achieve this is to have a writ-ten plan.

The concept of having a written plan for life or for use in guiding our daily activities may sound alien at first blush, but when you consider the importance of what you are dealing with (that is, getting what you want out of life), the preparation of a plan for life could well be the most important thing you ever do.

Many individuals expend time, effort, and money with attorneys, accountants, and advisors to devise their wills, which distribute their assets at death. The irony in this is that very few of these same individuals spend even a fraction of that time and energy deciding what they intend to have accomplished prior to the big event. Which is more important—how we deal with what we leave behind, or how we spend the life we have left to live? I vote for the latter.

In Sum . . .

♦ Maintaining momentum is a key to success and you can have it by always knowing what to do next—by always having a plan.

Planning Means Asking And Answering Questions

Generally speaking, planning is nothing more than asking questions and answering them. These three questions are the first ones to ask and answer:

1. Where am I now?
2. Where do I want to be?
3. What do I need to do to get from here to there?

These are good umbrella questions, but I would add four more to the initial list:

4. Why do I want to get "there" versus somewhere else? ("There" being any goal or objective.) This question raises the issue of whether we have selected the *right*

goal for ourselves. As Peter Drucker puts it, *it is better to do the right thing than to do things right.*

5. What is my motivation to get there? A corollary to this question is: Who do I want to prove this to and why?

6. What must I be willing to give up to get there? In other words, what sacrifices are required?

7. Am I prepared to make the commitment and endure the sacrifices?

In actuality, there are far more than just these seven questions to be answered in the process of planning anything significant.

In business planning, for example, I've developed a technique I call *Backward Business Planning* that others and I have used in hundreds of situations to drive the planning process. This is a question-and-answer technique at the core of which is over 300 questions and these questions drive the thinking so that end results are defined first, and then we define how we will achieve them. The feedback I consistently get from entrepreneurs, business managers, university professors, and business students who have used a book I wrote on this method is that the *questions* are the crown jewels to the process. One individual told me the questions were worth at least ten dollars apiece because asking the right question gets you halfway to the right answer. The other feedback I consistently receive is that *Backward Business Planning* works because it does just that, it starts at the end and works backwards.

> *I had six honest serving men—they taught me all I knew: Their names were Where and What and When—and Why and How and Who.*
>
> —Rudyard Kipling

In Sum . . .

♦ Planning means asking and answering questions and selecting the right questions will get you a good ways toward the answers.

Planning Your Life Is A Backward Process

Planning backwards doesn't apply just to business planning, it applies to planning in general and it certainly applies to planning our lives. That is, we begin at the end by defining what we want and then work backwards deciding what we need to do to get it—we define the desired effect, then figure out the required causes. There are seven steps involved:

1. Decide what you want to achieve by setting goals for each of the six aspects of your life: spiritual, family, mental, phys-

ical, social and career/financial. Make your choices and write them down, perhaps as in writing your epitaph.

2. Set a date and certain time for when you will achieve your goals. Goals without a certain date for their attainment are not goals, and they will not stimulate results.

3. Decide the significant accomplishments that have to be met between now and when your goals are achieved.

4. Think through the sacrifices you will have to make to achieve your goals and commit to making them.

5. Decide what resources will be required and where they can be obtained.

6. Organize the acquisition of resources and tasks into an orderly and logical manner, and establish interim goals along the way.

7. Stay flexible and revise as you go to meet changing conditions and to change directions toward new and revised goals.

These steps represent simple procedures conceptually, but it is not easy for everyone to implement these techniques at first. Don't let that stop you—the benefits of planning your life are enormous.

*In life it is possible to merely throw a heap of
stones together, but the pile is not beautiful.
We pyramid to the heights only when we lay
stone on stone according to a beautiful plan.*
          —W. N. Thomas

Take comfort in knowing that most people are
not steeped in experience in developing, implementing, and monitoring plans—especially plans for their
lives. Just relax, take it easy, and think it through.
Don't try to plan everything in your life all at once—I
recommend a modest beginning, followed by the evo-
lution and refinement of your life plans as you go
along.

*Have a bias toward action—let's see some-
thing happen now. You can break that plan
into small steps and take the first step right
away.*
        —Richard Thalheimer

An important aspect of all this planning is the
power that it creates. Planning is imaging to a large
degree, and imaging releases power because it builds
expectancy which will pull you toward success. You
also will begin to be pulled toward success as you
begin to define success in terms of goals.

I keep going back to the Chinese proverb that the
journey of a thousand miles begins with but a single
step because it offers much wisdom. However, the

thing to keep in mind is the end of the proverb—the *single step*. If you can't imagine that step, if you can't see yourself taking it, if you don't set a time and place to take that first step, you will never complete the journey.

Another thing to keep in mind is the totality of what you are creating—the big picture, so to speak. You can't have beauty without a beautiful plan, and what you are creating is a plan for a life with beauty in it.

In Sum . . .

♦ Planning releases the power of your imagination because it is impossible to plan toward goals without imagining their achievement.

♦ Planning is a backward process that re- quires defining your goals first, and then asking and answering questions about whether, how, and when they can be achieved. Planning is the Olympics of thinking.

The Glory Of Obstacles

An important point to consider is that obstacles are going to be encountered and plans will have to be altered from time to time. But, this isn't the bad news; it's the good news.

Without obstacles, there are no opportunities for growth. Our minds, our muscles, and our bodies grow and maintain their resilience and vitality only when we encounter resistance, and what is resistance if not an obstacle? Without obstacles, we would never summon our inner strength or rise to the occasion because there would never be an occasion to rise to. Thank goodness for obstacles.

The glory of obstacles is in the challenges and victories they afford. No general was ever great without having a great war to fight and great victories in it. Likewise, you will not rise to greatness unless you have mountains to climb. So don't let obstacles slow you down. Rather, let them be a comfort to spur you on.

> *View each obstacle in life as a little gift—open*
> *it and see what's inside.*
> —Mother Teresa (paraphrased)

Obstacles can't serve to spur you on, however, until you identify what they are, decide to deal with them, and develop and commit to a plan for doing so.

A word of caution here, however. As Samuel Johnson put it: *Nothing will ever be attempted if all possible obstacles must first be overcome.*

It is impractical to think through a solution to every possible problem before beginning. It also is a waste of time, for two reasons: First, the old cliche that we tend to make mountains out of mole hills is true. We envision obstacles to be more difficult than they are in actuality. This slows momentum and can kill enthusiasm—for no legitimate reason. Second, many obstacles will get out of our paths or be solved for us before we reach them.

Chloethiel Woodard Smith, a client of mine years ago who was a marvelous, award-winning architect, used to get so frustrated with many of her staff members when they would continually ponder matters, seek her advice, and otherwise put off getting things done. They seemed to her to be continually "debating the obstacles."

Mrs. Smith was up in her years when I met her, and I vividly remember my first luncheon with her, when she sipped her martini, dragged deeply on her unfiltered cigarette, and then put her attitude toward delay to me this way: "Young man, if you want to be successful in life, just do it! Why don't people just do it?"

A Message To Garcia, written by Elbert Hubbard, was published in 1899 and over 40 million copies were printed because of the power of the *just do it* message it contained. The story is about young Lieutenant Andrew Summers Rowan, who was called upon to deliver a message from President McKinley to a General Garcia in the hills of Cuba during the Spanish-American War.

When told of his assignment, Lieutenant Rowan did not ask numerous clarifying questions like who is General Garcia and how do I find him? He did not ask for a team of men to accompany him. He did not ask for special supplies or provisions.

Lieutenant Rowan did none of the typical things we all might expect; instead, he left without a word, made way by horse to Florida where he arranged a boat to Cuba. He penetrated Cuba days later, went into the mountains and delivered the message to General Garcia. He returned to the White House to inform the President that his mission had been accomplished. It took a few weeks, but Lieutenant Rowan just did it! He just did it!

Like Lieutenant Rowan, we, too, must *just do it* in life. There comes a time when choices and imagery must be set aside—there comes a time when we must act.

> *The great composer does not set to work because he is inspired, but becomes inspired because he is working. Beethoven, Wagner, Bach and Mozart settled down day after day to the job at hand with as much regularity as an accountant settles down with his figures. They didn't waste time waiting for inspiration.*
>
> —Ernest Newman

Individuals at a fair paid $25 to be raised 300 feet in a cage where they were supposed to leap out head first into the air—to be saved by the bungee cords attached to their ankles. We watched one fellow do this six times, and then we watched another individual go up in the cage and lose his nerve. As this second fellow was being lowered back down in the cage, the first jumper, the six-timer, said this to those standing nearby: *Why go to all the bother if you're not going to jump? The only way is to just do it, man. It's okay to scream, but just do it.*

Procrastination destroys more than what might have been done today. It can cause you to forego what might have otherwise been possible in a lifetime—a delay for even a day can alter an entire lifetime of accomplishments.

Begin it now. Just do it.

In Sum . . .

◆ We grow only because of the resistance we encounter.

◆ Choosing to have a happy day or to have success in life is not enough; you've got to go get it. Just do it.

Thunder is good, thunder is impressive; but it is lightning that does the work.
— Mark Twain

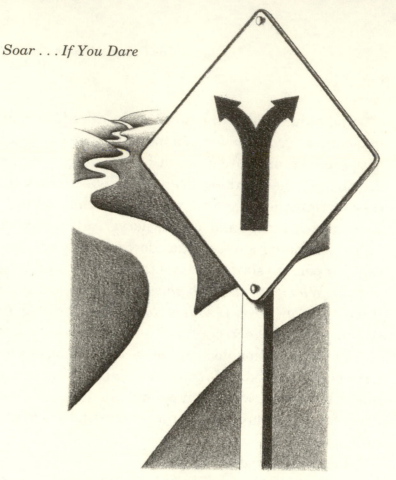

The Power Of Your Actions
What To Do . . .

1. Buy a ticket—get what you want in life by choosing to act.

2. Live with a bias to act—get into the action habit. Just do it.

3. Judge yourself not by what you say you will do, but by what you actually do.

4. Bite-size your beginnings into small, easily achievable steps. Begin by writing down what you will accomplish and the steps you will follow.

5. Set and commit to an exact time and place when you will begin and begin promptly.

6. *Write* down your long-term goals and your objectives so that you know what these are.

7. Resolve to create a plan to guide you in life, and then create it and implement it.

8. Know that with each obstacle you are becoming stronger and closer to success.

9. Just do it.

*Life is too short
to waste.
Dreams are
fulfilled only
through action,
not through
endless
planning to
take action.*
—David J. Schwartz

Seven

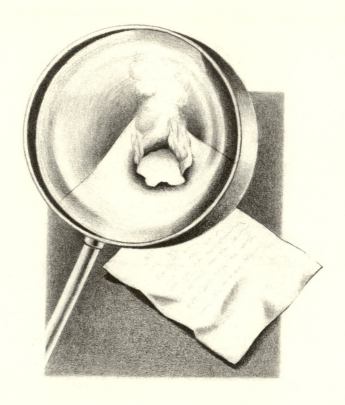

*Concentration is the magic you can use
to create supernatural power over
natural forces.*

The Power Of Your Concentration

YOUR POWER of concentration is released when you gather your physical and mental resources and focus them on a common objective. When a magnifying glass focuses sunlight toward a single spot on paper, the paper ignites, but until this focusing, this concentration of energy has occurred, nothing happens.

Unfortunately, most people live their lives without benefiting from the magic and the power of concentration. Peter Drucker, the business sage, observed this in the early 1960s when he wrote:

173

Concentration is the key . . . no other principle is violated as consistently as the basic principle of concentration . . . our motto seems to be let's do a little bit of everything.

The problem is that when we get wrapped up doing a little bit of everything, we tend to not do a lot of anything—and this leads to mediocrity and minimal accomplishments.

Individuals who use the power of concentration by design, intuition, or dumb luck are the people with the most, the biggest, and the greatest accomplishments in life, regardless of how accomplishments are defined. They also are the ones who have excelled in their fields. Those who have concentrated have been our greatest artisans, musicians, scientists, athletes, educators, statesmen, entertainers, spiritual leaders, authors—the list goes on.

> *Concentrate all your thoughts upon the work at hand. The sun's rays do not burn until brought into focus.*
> —Alexander Graham Bell

The power of concentration can be applied in all aspects of our lives in terms of resources and goals, but there is no instance where we can capitalize on the power of concentration more than we can in respect to our most precious, and in one sense, our only resource, *time.*

In Sum . . .

♦ A big difference in what we achieve results from differences in our powers of concentration and our ability to focus on a very few goals well done.

♦ Concentration is consistently violated by doing a little bit of everything.

♦ Concentration of resources is mostly the concentration of our lives—of our time.

Get The Power Of Concentration By Spending Your Time In Chunks

Years ago, I had the opportunity to see a training film on time management in which Peter Drucker had a secretary keep a log of how a busy executive spent every minute of his time for a week.

The results were amazing. The executive thought he had spent considerable time on important matters, but the secretary's log revealed that in actuality he had spent only a few minutes on several critical decisions.

The main messages were clear: The executive did not have control of his time; he did not spend his time as he had intended to; and he had no idea where his time was actually going.

Drucker offered several recommendations at the end of the training film, but the one that I have never forgotten and which is a crown jewel of wisdom is this: *Spend your time in chunks.*

Besides *time,* there are two operative words in Drucker's advice, and both deserve your attention: *spend* and *chunks.*

> *My definition of an educated person is one who can concentrate on one subject for more than two minutes.*
> —Robert A. Milikan

There are hundreds of millions of dollars invested each year on learning, teaching, and studying time management. Time management is a big business, but it's ironic that it is, and here's why: *There is no such thing as time management.*

There is no such thing as time management because we can't manage time, we can't create time, we can't slow it down, speed it up, expand it, or save it. There is only one thing we can do with time, and it is what Drucker said we can do, we can *spend* it.

Be avaricious of time; do not give any moment without receiving its value; only allow hours to go from you with as much regret as you give to your gold; do not allow a single day to pass without increasing the treasure of your knowledge and virtue.

—Le Tourneux

What we can manage is not time, but our spending of it. We can "manage our time" effectively only by spending it effectively. The way to do this is to plan your time expenditures in advance, and to plan your time expenditures in *chunks*.

A chunk of time is at least an hour. When you spend an hour on anything you are allowing your power of concentration to be released. Time spent on projects in ten-minute or even half-hour drabs and dribbles results in diffusion, not concentration.

To draw upon your power of concentration, spend your time in chunks of at least an hour, one chunk at a time, on one project at a time. Spending time in chunks is the key; the power this will release is truly amazing.

First and foremost let me establish an essential ground rule, however. Spending a one-hour chunk of time means spending a one-hour chunk of time *without interruptions*.

Until you develop some habits and techniques in this area, you likely are going to have difficulty spending time in uninterrupted chunks of at least an hour on anything. The reason is that most people are in the habit of spending time, as Drucker put it, doing a little bit of everything. These are tough habits to break because they have been ingrained for so many years and because the world around us does so much to reinforce continuation of the drab and dribble, do-a-little-bit-of-everything mentality.

The essential point that most people overlook, and the reason concentration is a *secret* power, is that unless you are consciously concentrating your attention and efforts for extended, uninterrupted periods, then what you are doing is about the same as focusing the magnifying glass for a second or two, and then moving it elsewhere. You may focus the magnifying glass often, but what is needed is not *often*—what is needed is all at once for an extended period until the paper ignites.

> *Spurts don't count.*
> —Herbert Kaufman

I recently observed this firsthand with my youngest daughter, who was studying for one of her courses in ten-to-fifteen minute drabs, in between phone calls, trips to the kitchen for a snack, and other assorted interruptions. Truth is, over a week's time, she had gotten nowhere to speak of. Then one day, I insisted she sit down and study in three uninterrupted one and one-half hour chunks, all in the same day—one in the morning, one at midday, and one in the evening. Even she was surprised with the results—when she was done studying in those three chunks, she was done! She took the exam and got a good grade. Why? Because she concentrated.

To illustrate the application of the power of concentration to your life on its broadest scale, let me ask you a question that may hit home. When was the last time you spent at least one solid *uninterrupted* hour just thinking about what you want out of life? Okay, if not an hour, when was the last time you spent an uninterrupted half-hour thinking about what you want out of life?

You may be the exception, but few people can honestly say that they *ever* have spent an uninterrupted hour thinking about their lives and goals. It should be no surprise then that most individuals aren't going to get what they want. They can pretty much expect to get out of life the kind of results my daughter would have gotten out of her exam had she not concentrated her thoughts and her actions.

One technique that helps ensure expending time in uninterrupted chunks is to plan for it by thinking through a time budget and adhering to it.

A time budget could go something like this. "Let me see, I'll get to the office and spend the first hour on the Acme proposal, then I'll spend an hour preparing reviews of my staff, then I'll get through my correspondence . . ." Or: "After dinner, I'll spend an hour thinking through my goals for next month and the images of those goals, and then . . ."

You get the point. Planning the expenditure of your time creates images of you spending your time, and once these images are created, you can create additional images of how you will not allow interruptions.

Before you know it, you will be spending time on what is important to you. You will have exercised choice over your time, chunks of it.

Time Bandits deserve special mention here because you simply must learn how to avoid them and fend them off. The objective is for *you* to decide how to spend your time, not to let someone or something else decide how to spend your time for you.

This means that when you are spending one of your important chunks of time, you should take special steps as a precaution to insulate yourself. One way is shut off your telephone, another is to close your door. An obvious technique you should not hesitate using is to tell people not to disturb you for an hour so you can concentrate. Whatever it takes, protect your chunks of time from interruptions.

This doesn't mean that you always will be alone when you are spending a chunk of your time. For example, I like to try and spend chunks of time with my daughters and my wife, and we often do this over an event, like dinner or an excursion. As another example, many businesses have scheduled weekly management team and staff meetings.

Although you will want to spend many of your chunks of time with others, it is often more advantageous to be alone—at least for an hour or more each day, and in some cases for several hours at a time.

However, it frequently is difficult to build up barriers to the Time Bandits in our lives. To deal with this, my recommendation is that everyone have a personal *hideaway*.

It is an experiment worth trying to be alone
and to be quiet for a brief period every day.
—Robert J. McCracken

Danielle Steel, one of the most prolific authors of our time, claims that she is able to be so productive only because she has a place to concentrate that she calls her hideaway. Steel's hideaway happens to be an entire separate residence, but most of us have to have different solutions.

A hideaway can be any place you can go hide and get away from the rest of the world for a chunk of time. I have several hideaways. One is the office at seven in the morning before everyone comes in. Another is a small study I use late at night when everyone has gone to bed. A third is a spot at the public library. Sometimes, I will even go have a cup of coffee in a hotel lobby, just to be alone. You can be "alone" with people around you so long as they don't take up your time or your thoughts.

The important thing is that *you* have someplace *you* can go. Find a hideaway that is right for you and use it.

In Sum . . .

♦ The one "time management" principle that is essential to know and apply is this one: Spend your time in uninterrupted chunks of an hour or so of your choosing.

♦ Get yourself a hideaway.

Concentration On A Limited Number Of Goals

Spending our time in chunks is essential for releasing the powers of concentration, but it is not all that is required. In addition, our efforts and attention must be narrowed and focused to a limited number of goals or projects at any one time. We must quit doing a little bit of everything, and start doing a lot of a few things, one thing at a time.

*I could never have done what I have done
. . . without the determination to concentrate
myself on one project at a time.*
—Charles Dickens

Concentration on one thing at a time has given us, besides the many works of Dickens, all of our great works of art, all of our great musical compositions, and all of our masterpieces in literature. Concentration on one thing at a time has provided us the light bulb, penicillin, the telephone, television, and every other invention known to man.

To quit doing a little bit of everything and start doing a few things well, we must consciously limit our goals and objectives. This means limiting long-term goals as well as short-term and intermediate goals. Limiting the targets in life is a practical recognition that we can't pursue everything and expect to get anything done.

While it is difficult to accept, the reality is that limiting goals means *eliminating* goals. Although some goals and objectives can be postponed, many must be completely eliminated. It is hard to turn one's back on a dream, but this must be done so that other dreams can be fulfilled. In fact, if this isn't done, you run the risk of spreading your efforts so thin that nothing gets done. We've all had days when this occurs, and you know how dissatisfied you are with the results.

He who wishes to fulfill his mission in the world must be a man of one idea, that is, one great overmastering purpose, overshadowing all of his aims, and guiding and controlling his entire life.

—Bate

Millions of individuals think they need to be good at several things in life to be successful, but quite the opposite is usually true—that is, to be successful you need to do only one thing in life well.

Doing one "thing" in life well certainly doesn't mean that we are incompetent in all other aspects of our lives—that's not the point. The point is that it is an easier and straighter road to success if we will just limit our attention to a few main goals in our lives at any one time. We can see where success has resulted from this kind of concentration in every facet of life imaginable. All of our great artists and entertainers mainly concentrate on their artistry or entertaining. Beethoven was into music most of the day, every day, and so is Garth Brooks, a recent rage in cross-over country music. The lives of all of our great athletes are dominated with sports—Michael Jordan eats, sleeps and thinks basketball.

Your mind is powerful enough to do more than one thing at one time, but you can only do one thing well at one time. Just do what you're doing while you're doing it.
—Ron Gilbert

In the business world, too, concentration leads to success. Xerox concentrated on xerography, and IBM concentrated on mainframe computers, and it was these concentrations that gave them their dominance and success.

Mars, the secretive candy manufacturer, provides another example of success through concentration and focus—this time on ingredients. Begin with a Three Musketeers that consists of nougat and chocolate, add caramel, alter the process slightly and now you have a Milky Way. Add peanuts and presto, you have a Snickers. Replace the light chocolate coating with dark chocolate and you now have a Milky Way Dark (formerly a Forever Yours). Then, remove the nuts from the Snickers, replace them with almonds, compress the nougat and what do you have? A Mars bar. Take the chocolate only, mould it into drops, spray it with a hard candy coating and you have M&Ms. Put a peanut inside (the same ones that go into the Snickers bar) and you have Peanut M&Ms.

I'm over simplifying of course, but Mars is successful in my view because the Mars family has concentrated on only a few ingredients, a few processes, and one major type of customer—people like you and me who like sweets and who want only the best.

Honda Motors is another example. Honda is beating General Motors in a game GM used to dominate and Honda is winning in part because it offers fewer than 20 models, whereas GM is still offering hundreds. Honda has the power of concentration on its side; GM doesn't.

The same principles that apply for our athletes, at Mars, and at Honda are just as applicable to your life and mine. We need to limit what we do so we have the opportunity to do one thing well. That one thing will carry us.

In addition to limiting the goals or projects you pursue, you should pursue them one at a time, an approach frequently referred to as dividing and conquering.

For example, if you divide big tasks into little ones and focus on the little tasks one at a time, you will get more done. An author who wants to write a work that is estimated to be about 100,000 words in length doesn't sit down and write it from start to finish. Instead, many authors set small goals, like 1,000 or 1,500 words per day; then in 60 to 100 days the overall task is done. Having numerous smaller goals provides the advantage that you always know what to do next, and knowing what to do next is a prerequisite for maintaining momentum.

A particular type of goal that should be divided in order to conquer is the obstacles you are in the process of overcoming. For example, it *may* work for someone to quit smoking, lose weight, and begin an exercise program all at once, but for most people challenges like these should be addressed one at a time.

In thinking through which goals you will or won't pursue, keep in mind the 80/20 tendency, which suggests that absent any effort on your part to change the relationship, 20% of your efforts will produce 80% of your results, and the other 20% of the results will consume the other 80% of your efforts.

In other words, we tend to spend most of our time and energies on tasks that are not so important, while leaving only a small portion of our time and energies for those that are. This being the case, we must take steps to consciously focus our energies and efforts so that the more important things in our lives get disproportionately *more* time and energy, not less.

We humans tend to do a lot of wheel spinning. This is partly because we don't spend time in chunks, but it also is partly because we have too many things going all at once and haven't given any consideration to which of our efforts are the ones producing the results.

One principal reason why men are so often useless is that they divide and shift their attention among a multiplicity of objects and pursuits.

—Nathaniel Emmons

For example, if you are spending only a few minutes each week visualizing the attainment of your goals in life, but considerably more time daydreaming about events in the past, then you need to look at this and modify your practices. The few minutes you do spend (your 20%) are accounting for 80% of what you will achieve. If you increase the time spent imaging the attainment of goals, you will achieve more.

Another crown jewel of advice I have had the fortune of reading came from a consultant called in to work with Andrew Carnegie years ago. The consultant was asked to provide advice as to how Carnegie could be more effective. The consultant said, so the story goes: "Start each day with a list of no more than five items to be accomplished. Put them in priority and work on only those items, in order, until they are completed. Do this every day of your life."

Carnegie followed the consultant's advice and found it so helpful that he sent the consultant a letter telling him it was the best advice he ever had, along with a check for $25,000! (*Success* magazine mentioned this story in its March 1992 issue and indicated the amount was $64,000—either way, it's a big sum.)

Do yourself a favor and adopt the advice that one man paid $25,000 to get. Start all of your days with a short list of "silver bullets," as I call them, no more than five items to be worked on. Then work on that list, in order, one item at a time. Your productivity will zoom.

To maximize the power of concentration, you must also concentrate the resources available to you. Concentration of resources is essential because the resources each of us has at our disposal are finite.

And herein lies the secret of true power. Learn, by constant practice how to husband your resources, and concentrate them, at any moment, upon a given point.
—James Allen

For instance, if you want big tomatoes, you should trim off the little shoots at the base of the tomato plants that drain off nutrients from the main stalks. When you snip off these "suckers," as they are called, the main shoots, and in turn the fruit, get plenty of water and food. But if you don't keep the plants pruned during their early stages, then you will end up with small tomatoes.

Or, let's say you have fifty tomato plants in your garden, but only enough water for ten plants a day.

What would you do? Would you take what little water you have and spread it over all fifty plants? Or would you water the plants on some kind of rotating basis, so that ten plants got a good soaking on one day, but on the other days they shriveled up from the heat?

If the objective is to have succulent tomatoes, then you had better select just ten plants and water those same ten plants each and every day, while letting the others go. The hard part is letting the others go, but the reality is that you simply do not have enough water.

> *As the gardener, by sheer pruning, forces the sap of the tree into one or two vigorous links, so should you stop off your miscellaneous activity and concentrate your forces on one or two points.*
> —Ralph Waldo Emerson

The water for your tomato plants is just the metaphor for your time, your money, your physical efforts, and all of your other resources. Don't sprinkle your resources over too many plants in your life. Pick a few and feed them well. You'll get big results.

In Sum . . .

◆ You only need do one thing truly well to be successful in life.

◆ Doing a little bit of everything is the quickest and surest road to failure.

◆ Concentration is essential because resources, particularly time, are finite, and you never know when they might run out.

◆ Limiting your goals means eliminating your goals—not all of them, but some.

Concentration and Persistence

Never give up, for that is just the place and time that the tide will turn.
—Harriet Beecher Stowe

Persistence and perseverance are fundamental aspects of concentration. You must concentrate your resources, efforts, and attention over extended periods of time to get real results. In many cases, the extended period of time is the rest of your life.

In imaging, for example, it is not enough to create and hold images in your mind only once in a while. You must review your images many times a day, every day, forever. Your goals and the images of your goals may change, but the habit of creating and holding images must never stop. Your mind will achieve its greatest breakthroughs only after it has had the advantage of sustained concentration.

As Winston Churchill said: *Never, never, never quit.* It is sad, but millions of individuals do quit, and often they stop just a little bit short of their goals. This is like digging in a gold mine for months and stopping when your last pick stroke was only a fraction of an inch away from the mother lode you sought. You must push through until you get breakthrough.

You didn't learn to ride a bicycle by trying a few times and quitting. You learned by staying on until you could ride. When that breakthrough came, you rolled along without falling. It is hard to imagine not being able to ride a bicycle after the learning task is done.

> *There is no sudden leap into the stratosphere . . . There is only advancing step-by-step, slowly and tortuously up the pyramid of your goals.*
>
> —Ben Stein

The same is true of making that big sale, getting that A on an examination, winning that job, writing that book, and doing anything else in life the first time. The difference between having done the deed and not is all the difference in the world, but it could be just an inch or two away. What is needed is persistence.

Thomas J. Watson, the founder of IBM, said: *Would you like me to give you a formula for . . . success? It's quite simple, really. Double your rate of failure.*

All too often we have the wrong perspective on failure. Failure is not bad per se, in fact failure and learning from failure is usually a prerequisite to success. To think that you will be successful on your first, your second, or even your tenth attempt at anything simply is inconsistent with the way much of the world works, and here are some examples to drive home the point:

> Orville Redenbacher experimented for years until he came up with what we now all know as Orville Redenbacher Gourmet Popping Corn—the best-selling popcorn in the world.

> *The Thorn Birds, Gone With The Wind,* and literally hundreds and hundreds of masterpieces in literature were rejected dozens and dozens and dozens of times before they were finally accepted for publication.

> *An Officer and a Gentleman, Platoon,* and hundreds of other extremely successful movies were turned down, sometimes as often as 100 times, before they were accepted.

Eddie Arcaro, the champion jockey, lost his first 45 races.

Michael Jordan was cut from his high school basketball team.

Bobby Bonilla, the highest paid player in baseball with a five-year, $29 million Mets contract, was initially passed over by each and every one of the 26 major league teams.

When people are successful, we tend to know only of their wins, but those wins always come about because of attempts where wins weren't always achieved. Babe Ruth and Hank Aaron are excellent examples. Ruth had 714 home runs and Hank Aaron had 755 home runs in their respective careers. Those are terrific records, but what we often ignore is that to get them, Ruth was at bat 8,399 times and Aaron was at bat 12,364 times and both Ruth and Aaron struck out almost twice as many times as they hit home runs. There was a lot of swinging going on.

Try and try again is a theme in life and a rule of success not because we have to fail before we can win, but because we have to learn from our failures and because the golden ring isn't always there for us to grab exactly when we want to grab it. Sometimes we have to be patient and wait until it is our time to shine—a time when the conditions are right for us to get breakthrough.

We live in a world of instant everything, and this "programs" us into expecting instant results in all aspects of our lives. We have instant coffee, instant entertainment by the click of a switch, nearly instant pizza in thirty minutes or less, and instant receipts at the instant pump-your-own gas pump. With all this instantaneous delivery, we come to expect instant results in every other part in our lives. Why not, right?

Unfortunately, life does not work that way. We can't get a new baby in one month, it takes nine; we can't acquire new habits overnight, it takes several months; and we can't expect to achieve our major successes in life on an instant time frame.

My own experience has been that it has taken me about three to five years of concentrated, sustained effort to acquire each of my major skills. It took me four or so years to really know what I was doing in the public accounting world; it took me several years of working in the venture capital business before I had an in depth grasp of things; and I have been writing a chunk or two each day now for over five years. So there does seem to be a pattern, at least to my own skill developments.

The important point to remember is that it takes a while to get good at anything, and it takes a while to get worthwhile results—that's why perseverance, in many cases for years and years, is required.

Nothing in the world can take the place of persistence. Talent will not; nothing is more common than unsuccessful men with talent. Genius will not; unrewarded genius is almost a proverb. Education will not; the world is full of educated derelicts. Persistence and determination alone are omnipotent.
— Calvin Coolidge

We are not beaten when we have swung a hundred times at the ball and not hit it—we are beaten only when we fail to swing again. This kind of sustained swinging requires concentration in every manner you can conceive it, and it requires continuing until you get the results you really want to have.

In Sum . . .

♦ Rest, recharge yourself, evaluate, change courses and alter plans as needed, but never, never, never quit.

♦ Accept your failures as milestones necessary for success.

———

Concentration is the factor that causes the great discrepancy between men and the results they achieve . . . the difference in their power of calling together all the rays of their ability and concentrating on one point.
—Orison Swett Marden

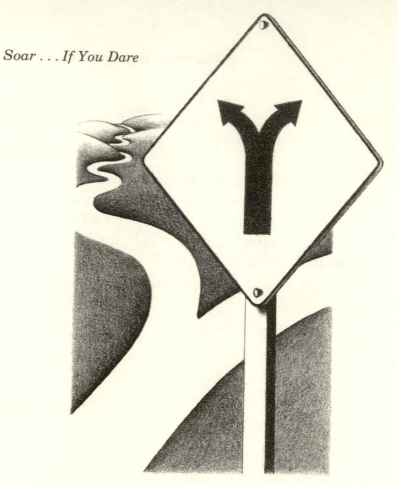

The Power Of Your Concentration

What To Do . . .

1. Constantly limit your activities and your goals so that you are concentrating your resources and energies.

2. Consciously decide how you will spend your time (that is, your life). Adopt the chunk-of-time expenditure *habit* instead of the habit of doing everything a little at a time in drabs and dribbles.

3. Get a hideaway.

4. Learn to say NO to Time Bandits.

5. Limit your goals by eliminating goals and then prioritizing those that remain.

6. Focus on one task at a time.

7. Begin each day with a list of your "silver bullets"— the five most important things you want to accomplish—then work your list.

8. Recognize that it frequently takes longer and requires more energy, time, and resources than was perceived at the outset—but don't let this stop you—persist until you succeed.

9. Never, never, never quit.

*Nothing can
add more
power to your
life than
concentration.*
—Nido Qubein

Eight

*Your habits are the root systems in your
life. You can change what you will
become and what you will accomplish
only by first changing your habits.*

The Power Of Your Habits

ARISTOTLE, the great Greek philosopher wrote: *You are what you repeatedly do*. What we repeatedly do, of course, is what becomes our habits. And, as Nathaniel Emmons, the theologian, put it: *Habit is either the worst of your enemies or the best of your servants*.

Make no mistake about it. Your habits are one or the other. Your habits are either your servants serving up success or your enemies defeating you at every turn—no matter how hard you try.

This year, millions of people will be defeated by their habits and thereby fail to change some aspect of their lives. Some will fail to lose weight permanently; others will fail to quit smoking; and still others will fail to accomplish some personal goal—maybe such as painting a picture, learning a new language, or achieving a career milestone.

But not everyone fails. Millions of people do quit smoking or lose weight permanently, and millions more achieve numerous and varied goals in their family, business, and social lives.

Why is there this disparity? Why do so many people fail to achieve what they set out to do, whereas others have success?

The answer has to do with the secret power of habits and the ability individuals have to choose the habits that make up their lives. To explore the amazing phenomenon of habit power, let's look at the garden of life and imagine that we want to replace unsightly, snarly weeds with flowers.

First, we have to recognize that there is more to our garden than meets the eye. Above the ground are the parts of the flowers and the weeds that we can see, and beneath the ground are the seeds and root systems that comprise the garden's base. We can't permanently change what we see growing until we first change the seeds and the roots below the ground. A weed chopped off above ground will continually come back until we dig its roots out of the soil—we need to get beneath the surface and change the source.

The source of success is found not in the part of our gardens that we can see—rather, it lies in the root systems beneath the surface. Efforts directed only to the parts of our lives above the ground are doomed at the outset because it is the root systems we need to change—the root systems called habits.

In Sum . . .

♦ You are what you repeatedly do—you have become your habits, and to change yourself, you must change your habits.

♦ Millions fail to achieve what they want because they don't look beneath the surface of their actions and alter the roots of their habits.

♦ You will not be able to effect major changes in your life without changing your habits.

The Evolution Of Habits And Their Root Systems

You began life with no habits. As the years passed, you picked up many habits along the way so that now you are a creature of the habits you have learned. You brush your teeth in the morning. You skip breakfast, or you eat pretty much the same breakfast over and over. In school or seminar settings you prefer a seat in a certain section of the room, and you either take notes or don't. You usually sit in the same general section in movie theaters. In the evenings, you may watch television, read books or take a class. It may seem that you vary what you do, but in reality patterns of habits exist and all of these combined make up the big habit of our lives.

You didn't necessarily consciously choose to have each of your habits, but regardless of where they came from, they now control your life—perhaps more appropriately, they are your life.

The bad habits in our lives are the weeds in our gardens with elaborate mental root systems beneath the surface.

For this reason, individuals who want to quit smoking but who only chop off the visible part of their habits will fail. To quit smoking, one must also deal with the habit root systems beneath the ground, such as having a cigarette after each meal; having a cigarette with a cup of coffee; having a cigarette upon awakening; having a cigarette while reading or working; having a cigarette with a drink . . . and so on. Smoking is not just one habit; it comprises many individual habits, and each of these must be dealt with.

All habits do not produce weeds, of course. Many habits, the servants in our lives, produce beautiful flowers.

One of your servants could be the habit of briskly walking after dinner each evening. Another habit might be spending time in chunks instead of drabs and dribbles. And another good habit could be visualizing the attainment of your goals before going to sleep.

We each have dozens, and maybe even hundreds of habits, some good, some not so good, some bad, but the point is we have them and we have become them. Therefore, if we want to change what we have become, we must begin by changing our habits. And we might as well change all of our habits into good ones since that is what we will become.

Habit, my friend, is practice long pursued,
that at last becomes the man himself.
—Evenus

The reason people fail to change themselves is not because they don't want to, or because they don't try. People fail to achieve what they want because it doesn't dawn on them that they need to dig deeper, weed out bad habits at their roots, and plant good new habits in fresh, weed-free soil.

Cutting down a weed is not so good as uprooting it.

—Selwyn G. Champion

To change yourself, you must *consciously* change your habits, and when you understand and begin to apply this seemingly simple concept, you understand and are applying one of the truly secret powers of success.

Keep in mind, however, that changing one's habits takes a while, so don't get discouraged if a new habit doesn't seem to stick right away. Experts say it takes four to six months to adopt an exercise program as a habit, and it may take this long or longer for mental imaging techniques to become ingrained. Do not despair if results don't come right away. Prepare yourself mentally for the time frame expected. Long-term rewards surely will provide the payoff you expect when you plan your efforts.

In Sum . . .

♦ To effect a positive and permanent change in your life, you must first plant and cultivate one or more positive and permanent new habits. That's the secret power of habit.

How To Use Your Secret Power
Of Habit For Success

J. Paul Getty, one of the wealthiest industrialists in the early 1900s, attributed much of his success to the attention he paid to developing and pruning his habits. He wrote: *. . . to reach the top . . . the individual must be quick to break those habits that can break him—and hasten to adopt those practices that will become the habits that help him achieve the success he deserves.*

You can read all the self-help, inspirational and motivational books you can find, you can listen to all the self-help audio tapes you can get your hands on, you can seek all manner of wisdom and advice from others, and you can take steps to implement what you have learned. But all of this will be a total and absolute waste of time unless you apply your knowledge to changes in your habits. Let me repeat that because it is so absolutely essential: *You must apply what you learn toward changes in your habits.*

The understanding and control of our habits are not only key ingredients for success, but they also are the yeast in the bread. To get what you want out of life, figure out the habits you will need to get you there and then figure out which of your habits are obstacles in the road to be removed.

To know what your habits are, write them down so you can identify which of your habits are working to your advantage and which are not, then develop and implement a game plan for change.

It is never easy to change a habit, and the longer you've had one, the more difficult the task is going to be. As Mark Twain put it: *Habit is habit and not to be flung out of the window by any man but coaxed down stairs a step at a time.* Twain's quote can certainly pertain to acquiring a good habit, as well as eliminating a bad habit. We can't catapult a new, good habit from one landing to another, we must coax it *up* stairs, a step at a time.

There is a poem that describes the task of changing a habit quite well:

> *"How shall I a habit break?"*
> *As you did that habit make.*
> *As you gathered, you must lose.*
> *As you yielded, now refuse.*
> *Thread by thread the strands we twist*
> *Till they bind us neck and wrist.*
> *Thread by thread the patient hand*
> *Must untwine ere free we stand.*
> —John Boyle O'Reilly

Like O'Reilly, many others have used a thread metaphor to explain habits because it describes a pattern of habits learned through repetition.

Tryon Edwards was quoted as saying: *Any act often repeated soon forms a habit; and habit allowed, steadily gains in strength. At first it may be but a spider's web, easily broken through, but if not resisted it soon binds us with chains of steel.*

Chains of steel do not loosen easily. Enormous, consistent effort is required. And something else is required: repetition. It doesn't matter how long a habit has been in existence or how strong it is, it can be replaced. This doesn't mean it's easy—it means it's possible.

The *first* step in adopting a new habit or breaking an old habit is to recognize that we can*not* adopt or break our habits, we can only *ex*change them.

Our habits preoccupy every minute of every day; there is no such thing as a void of habits. Therefore, you can't acquire any new habits without replacing old ones, *and* you can't get rid of any old habits unless you fill their void with new habits.

> *A nail is driven out by another nail; habit is overcome by habit.*
>
> —Erasmus

For example, to get into the habit of spending your time in chunks, you must get out of the habit of spending time in drabs and dribbles. Similarly, to lose weight, you must replace existing eating habits with new ones, such as reaching for a piece of fruit. And if you want to get into the habit of reading a book a little each night to stimulate your mind, then you'll need to exchange your current evening habits—maybe such as watching TV.

A common mistake many of us make is to expect too much too fast. With habits, it is better to begin small and ensure constant repetition than to begin in a big spurt that is not sustainable. If you want to spend your time in chunks, don't expect to be able to transform yourself overnight. Begin perhaps by trying to set aside just one "chunk" of time per day. When that's a habit, set aside your next chunk.

After being prepared to exchange habits, the *second* step in adopting a new one is to make the commitment to put forth the effort required to repeat the new habit until it is "learned" or becomes acquired. You also need to commit to putting forth the maintenance effort required to sustain the new habit for a lifetime. That's right, for a lifetime.

We seem to have a propensity to acquire undesirable habits more readily than we do good habits. The acquisition of good habits seems to always require more from us. It is easier to get into the habit of sleeping in than it is to get into the habit of going for a jog each morning. It is easier to get into the habit of overeating than it is to get into the habit of eating well. Part of this is because many external factors influencing bad habits are convenient (as in fast food chains), temporarily pleasing (as in video games and smoking), or just plain easy (as in TV).

Because of those factors, it is important at the outset to understand the mental commitment required to acquire (exchange) habits. For example, if you are going to adopt a morning jogging habit, then think through the sustained commitment required to make jogging your morning habit. Are you really ready to commit to jogging every morning for life? If not, think through the commitment you are prepared to make, perhaps such as going for a walk three nights a week.

The *third* step in exchanging one habit for another is to identify, specifically, what you will be exchanging. Begin by summarizing all aspects of the existing habit to be replaced—it's like seeing an X-ray of the root systems in your habit garden. After you know what you are going to replace, then describe what the new habit or habits will be. Writing down the details is essential.

The *fourth* step is to develop a plan for implementation and a related series of images in which you see yourself repeating the pattern of the new habit in exchange for the old habit. The key is to know *in advance* exactly how you are going to handle every major situation you can imagine encountering. Planning and thinking through a habit exchange in this level of detail is a lot of work. But to exchange one major habit for another it is essential because it provides the preconditioning and forethought needed to head off old habit patterns.

For example, to change your eating habits, think through your handling of the situations that are going to give you trouble. If you have been in the lifelong habit of eating double helpings of your mother's cooking just to please her, then figure out what you are going to do when she says, "Have another piece, dear." Imagine and practice mentally what you are going to say instead of falling back onto your standby habit of smiling and handing her your plate.

If you are going to get into the habit of going for a walk after dinner instead of vegetating in front of the TV, then think through precisely what you will do when inclement weather arrives—will you go back to your old TV habit days, will you go out into the rain anyway, or will you do something entirely different? What will you do? Think it through; then you can avoid backsliding.

A young man I know used to get Cs and Ds in school and occasionally an F in math. He was passing, but barely. His parents sent him to a course where he learned how to study. This course helped him acquire some new habits: the habit of taking notes in class, the habit of reviewing his notes a little each day even if he had no assignments, the habit of talking out loud to explain to himself what he was learning, and numerous others. The cumulative results of all these new study habits was remarkable. After learning these new study habits, the young man never got less than a B in any class—including his math courses, where he became a straight A student!

No habit will continue to survive if it is not fed or reinforced periodically. Periodic reinforcement is important for all habits, but it is particularly important when we are adopting brand-new habits that are quite different from what we are used to.

New seeds in any garden need tender loving care, and the keys to this are moderation and consistency. New seeds don't need a ton of fertilizer and buckets of rain all at once—what they need is a gentle sprinkling each and every day and a little fertilizer once in a while. These same principles apply to new habits. If you are going to begin a lifelong exercise program and have never exercised previously, then begin modestly and follow up with periodic care and constant reinforcement.

> *The beginning of a habit is like an invisible thread, but every time we repeat the act we strengthen the strand, add to it another filament, until it becomes a great cable and binds us irrevocably through and through.*
> —Orison Swett Marden

One way to care for and reinforce a new habit is to maintain charts and daily journals that pace and track progress. Another reinforcement technique is to place reminders where you see them often—like taping a supportive quote on your bathroom mirror or on the corner of your desk. These will do wonders.

Physical reminders are excellent, but mental reminders are vital as well. You must reinforce the adoption of new patterns with imaging, and you must image often each day, particularly just before retiring.

If you visualize the "new you" applying your newly acquired habits at bedtime, then that is the you that will wake up in the morning. If you take a few moments to imagine the new you each morning, then that is the you that will go on into the day. And so on. But the moment you stop imaging the new you, look out, for the images of the old you in the grooves of your brain will bleed through. Old images of bad habits, unfortunately, *are never completely erased—* they are just covered over with new images that must constantly be repeated.

It is said that once a smoker, always a smoker, once an alcoholic, always an alcoholic, once an over-eater, always an overeater, and so on. I believe this and can attest to it. I quit smoking for twelve years once and started right back up again when I had a single cigar. I have since quit smoking again, but I know now to never have that next smoke.

I wish I could write that old images of "good" habits are just as easy to retrieve, but I don't think that's so. I think that once we allow ourselves to acquire a new "bad" habit in exchange for an old "good" habit, the good habit does not re-emerge readily—it must once again be coaxed up the steps.

In Sum . . .

♦ We don't actually "acquire" new habits or "break" old habits. Rather, we exchange one habit for another—we make the choices as to what we exchange.

♦ There is no such thing as an absence of habits. Some habit will always fill a void created when a habit is discarded.

♦ Habits need reinforcement to grow and sustain themselves.

Your Attitude Habits

Nothing will affect the outcome of your life more than your *attitude* toward it; and although you may not have thought about it in this light before, your attitude is the result of the physical and mental habits you have learned over the years.

If you tend to be a happy, enthusiastic person, it is because you have a root system of positive attitude habits to support you each day. You likely smile a lot, walk with a spring in your step and look for the best in people. But if you typically are down in the dumps, it is because of the down-in-the-dumps attitude habits you have acquired over the years, all of which can and should be changed. You can quit frowning and adopt a smiling habit instead.

What is your standard response when people ask how it's going? Are you in the habit of saying, "Great!" and meaning it? Or are you in the habit of rolling your eyes and saying, "I wish you hadn't asked?"

Just by changing the habit of what you say when people ask, you will have begun to change the kind of days you will have. Your physical actions, even if forced at first by sheer will power, sooner or later will begin to affect your attitude.

I called a friend who had lost tens of millions of dollars in real estate, and still he bubbled cheerfully when he answered the telephone. I asked him how he kept such an upbeat attitude. His answer was unexpected. He said he never complains about not having shoes because he knows that some people don't even have feet. My friend keeps life in perspective, and he chooses to have a positive attitude at all times. He maintains his positive attitude by having a positive response habit—he says he's doing great and, as a result, he is.

In Sum . . .

♦ Nothing will affect the outcome of your life more than your attitude toward it.

Your Self-Talk Habits

There is one person you talk to and listen to more than anyone else, and that person is you. The words you say to yourself each day number in the tens of thousands, and what you say, how you say it, and the tone of your inner voice constitute your self-talk attitude habit.

This inner speech, your thoughts, can cause you to be rich or poor, loved or unloved, happy or unhappy, attractive or unattractive, powerful or weak.

—Ralph Charell

There have been a number of books on self-talk, one even entitled *What To Say When You Talk To Yourself* by Shad Helmstetter. The main message of these books is that what we say to ourselves all day long is *reaching* and *repeating* into our minds. What reaches and repeats onto the crystal walls of our subconscious minds does become our realities.

Any message reaching our subconscious minds will be accepted if it is repeated often enough. The advertising gurus on Madison Avenue have written books on this technique and it has been proven to work time and again.

It doesn't matter what the message is, and it doesn't matter whether the message is actually true; as long as the message is feasible, from a trusted source, and repeated often, our subconscious minds will accept it as true and implement it accordingly.

This being the case, we ought to listen carefully to what we say to ourselves because we trust ourselves so much and because we repeat more messages to ourselves than we can ever imagine. For example, have you ever said something similar to any of these?

"I'm not good at chemistry."

"I'm a poor driver."

"I'm just meant to be fat."

"I feel tired all the time."

"I'm not good with foreign languages."

"I'm just a smoker at heart."

"I could never speak in front of groups."

W. Clement Stone said that *self-suggestion makes you master of yourself*. Self-suggestion also can make you a slave of yourself if your self-talk habits are negative like those above. If you are in the habit of saying you are tired all the time, your subconscious mind says, "Okay, I'm tired," and then it goes about implementing the order. If you are in the habit of saying, "I'm fat," that is what your subconscious mind will accept and implement. While our bodies may be fat, that fat begins in our heads.

The point is this: Our subconscious mind does not evaluate what we say in our habitual self-talk; it accepts whatever we say as true, and then goes about implementing it.

While we can change our self-talk habits to whatever we want them to be, there is a caveat: Our self-talk must be believable. In other words, if you weigh three hundred pounds, it won't do any good to get into the habit of saying, "I'm skinny" all day long to yourself because you won't believe that; but it would work if you were taking steps to lose weight and supplemented those steps with self-talk like, "I am becoming trim." This indeed would be both believable and reinforcing to the physical habits you are acquiring.

A subtlety that exists with self-talk is that it should be in the *present* tense; that is, it is *not* productive to self-talk in the future tense such as, "I'm going to become a millionaire" or "I'm going to become thin." Instructions to the subconscious mind are taken only one way, and that is literally. If you are *going* to become a millionaire or become thin, then that means you aren't a millionaire now and you aren't thin now, so there is no work for your subconscious to do now. This being the case, your subconscious mind will put off becoming a millionaire until tomorrow, which of course never comes. An alternative would be to say, "I am becoming a millionaire," or "I am becoming thinner." This is both believable and in the present tense.

As another example, if you aren't getting good grades or if you aren't making the progress in your career that you desire, it would be like throwing seeds on stone to say, "I'm getting great grades" or "I'm on a fast track at work." Again, you just won't believe it. But you could say, "I am becoming a better student," or "I am becoming a more valuable employee." Both of these should be readily believable if you are putting forth any reasonable efforts at all.

Think of your self-talk as a constant barrage of radio commercials that you can't turn off, but that you can repeat and revise to your liking and to your advantage.

The power of reprogramming your self-talk habits is truly amazing. If you get into the habit of getting up in the morning and saying to yourself, "I am going to have a great day," chances are you will. If you get into the habit of saying to yourself, "I am achieving my goal of . . ." you will move closer to its achievement.

Get into the habit of allowing yourself only positive self-talk. If you are not used to having a positive conversation with yourself all day long, this habit will take some time to adopt, but the rewards will be tremendous.

In Sum . . .

♦ We become what we think about all day long. Our self-talk is the audio expression of our thoughts. To alter what you think (and thereby alter what you are), alter what you say to yourself.

Personal Imaging Habits

Somewhere along the way, you have acquired imaging habits that now collectively portray to you your own visions of yourself, including visions of your personal self-esteem and your deservedness. You may not readily be consciously aware of what these images are, but you have them just the same, and it is essential that you change these images if they are anything but positive.

If your self-*talk* habits are radio commercials,

then your self-*imaging* habits are television commercials, and they are that much more powerful.

> *Change the self-image and you change the personality and the behavior. "Self-image" is the key to human personality and human behavior.*
>
> —Maxwell Maltz

The habits of how you see yourself are crucial because those repeating images are what you are or what you are becoming. If you visualize yourself as timid, overweight, or unsuccessful, then what you are doing is playing a commercial of you in these roles. These you must change, for these you will become.

> *The brain simply believes what you tell it most. And what you tell it about you, it will create. It has no choice.*
>
> —Marilyn Grey

Denis E. Waitley, author of *The Psychology of Winning,* wrote: *Relentless, repetitive self-talk is what changes our self-image.* This means that to change your self-image, you have to get into the *daily habit* of forcing yourself to play positive images of you— actual, detailed visualizations of the assertive, trim, successful you that you have chosen to be and that you are becoming.

In Sum . . .

◆ The you that you see in your mind is the you that you are becoming. If you don't like the picture on the screen, change the channel.

Imaging Daily Goal Achievement

Hand-in-hand with your images of yourself are the images of you achieving your goals. What you must do is get into the habit of holding images in your mind of your goals being attained. These images must be repeated over and over daily, each and every day. Most importantly, your goal achievement images must be reviewed just before retiring and first thing upon arising. These are critical habits to get into.

Your morning thoughts may determine your conduct for the day. Optimistic thoughts will make your day bright and productive . . .
—William M. Peck

The keys to this are to take a few moments just before retiring and again just upon arising to imagine what you will achieve for the day. Don't start daydreaming and fall asleep right away at night. Force yourself to stay awake two-to-three more minutes and think about and imagine your accomplishments as they unfold the next day. Then do the same thing upon arising. Do not jump out of bed when the alarm goes off. Sit up in bed two or three minutes, close your eyes, and visualize what you intend to do during the day. See yourself completing the tasks you desire to complete for the day. These few minutes or so each day, a small investment in truth, will reward you manyfold.

The importance of daily imaging can't be over-emphasized. Even though we're talking about habits consuming only about five minutes a day in total, I know that only a very small percentage of readers is going to take the time and effort to conceive, adopt, and implement a series of daily imaging habits. I also know that those who do will first see their dreams in their mental images, and then they will see their dreams come true, and those who don't, won't.

In Sum . . .

◆ You will achieve your goals only if they are foremost in your mind, and the way to get them there is through positive, goal-oriented imaging habits.

Thoughts lead on to purposes; purposes go forth in action; actions form habits; habits decide character; and character fixes our destiny.

—Tryon Edwards

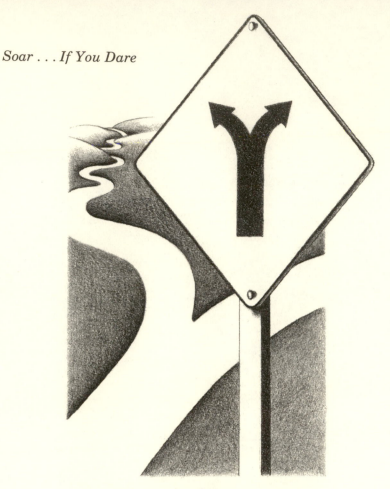

The Power Of Your Habits

What To Do . . .

1. After deciding what you want out of life, list the positive habits you must acquire to get you there and list the undesirable habits you must lose along the way.

2. Commit to changing your habits for the better and develop plans by specifying in writing the precise habits you will acquire in exchange for those you will abandon. Think through the details, know in

advance how you will handle difficulties that surely will stand in your way—visualize yourself overcoming the obstacles, visualize yourself in your new habits.

3. Create and use habit reinforcements such as charts, reminders, and supportive quotes.

4. Acquire positive attitude habits—view life in the most positive way possible, choose to be happy instead of sad, choose to be positive instead of negative.

5. Acquire positive self-talk habits—check your self-talk and change it for the better.

6. Acquire positive self-imaging habits; decide how you want to be and begin imagining the new you.

7. Acquire habits of continually visualizing the achievement of your goals—see yourself achieving your goals through your efforts.

Sow an act . . .
reap a habit
sow a habit . . .
reap a character;
sow a character . . .
reap a destiny.

—George Dana Boardman

Nine

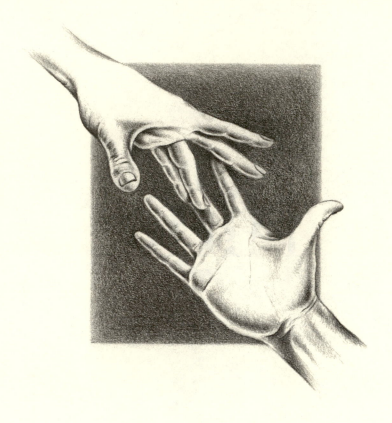

Love is the greatest and most powerful of all your secret powers. It is your love that can move the mountains.

Your Ultimate Secret Power

A MAN returned to the store with his newly purchased chain saw and complained that it took him over an hour of arduous work to cut down each tree he attacked with the saw. This naturally baffled the store owner so he went into the woods with the man to try the machine for himself. When the store owner pulled on the cord of the chain saw it started up with a loud roar. Scowling, the man said: "What's that noise?"

Love is not something we tend to think of in terms of its power, yet trying to achieve success in life without turning on your love is like sawing away at a tree without starting your chain saw—you might hack through, but not very easily—and why would you want to flail away anyway, when you could slice through with no strain at all in a fraction of the time?

Og Mandino, a businessman who has been successful in many endeavors, including as publisher of *Success* magazine, wrote *The Greatest Salesman In The World,* a best-seller which has been translated into many languages. I have given this wonderful book as a gift to dozens of individuals and I recommend it highly. What I found surprising given the title of Mandino's book, is that a key part of it centers on the power of love.

Before reading this book, I had never drawn a direct correlation between love and business. Since then, I have changed my attitude. I now know that behind every successful person is a driving, roaring force called love.

The part I like most in Mandino's book is the scrolls he works into his story, and my favorite is the Scroll marked II, which begins:

I will greet this day with love in my heart. For this is the greatest secret of success in all ventures. Muscle can split a shield and even destroy life itself but only the unseen power of love can open the hearts of man and until I master this act I will remain no more than a peddler in the market place. I will make love my greatest weapon and none on who I call can defend upon its force . . . my love will melt all hearts liken to the sun whose rays soften the coldest day.

—Og Mandino

Love is not a word that is in common use in business, academic, or other settings, and James A. Autry, president of the Meridith Corporation's magazine group and author of *Love & Profit—The Art of Caring Leadership* points this out in his book. He relates this story about his boss, Bob Burnett: *Bob was the first man I ever heard use the word 'love' as an attribute of someone in business. It was . . . in a speech to managers, on the subject of self-renewal. The reaction in the room was palpable, almost one of shock, and at the time I marveled at how gutsy Bob was in just saying the word. Apparently it did not hurt his career. He became president and chief executive officer of Meridith Corporation, and now is chairman of the board.* The existence of love and its powerful effects are ever-present in all aspects of life if we only take a moment to pause and observe.

I had the opportunity to know a remarkable man, Jack Whitehead, who recently passed away after a life full of accomplishments. Jack helped found *Research!* America which promotes biomedical research, he amassed a fortune in his lifetime in business endeavors, and he shared his wealth with others, such as his $135 million gift to the Massachusetts Institute of Technology.

But his wealth transcended money. At a board of director's meeting of Digene Diagnostics, Inc., a company in the DNA diagnostics field, Jack made a small comment that paints a big picture of how rich he was in his heart.

We were evaluating selling techniques for DNA probes that categorize cancer types when someone suggested that we figure out a way for doctors to make more money from the probes, since doctors, who would be ordering them, would order more if they made more.

To this, Jack shook his head, responding slowly, softly, but with thunder: "Well, if you believe in the tooth fairy, that's not the right answer, is it? We should make the best product we can for the lowest possible price, and let the doctors worry about themselves."

Here was a man with a fresh red carnation in his

lapel, a man worth hundreds of millions of dollars, a man successful beyond the wildest dreams of most people—yet here, too, was a man who still believed in the tooth fairy—not literally, but in the benevolent sense, the sense of love. Here was a man who was so full of love that it affected his feelings for his customers, though anonymous and unknown, he loved them and he wanted them to get good medicine at fair prices.

Someone said at Jack's funeral that there are two types of people, the givers and the takers, and Jack Whitehead was a giver. The heart and soul of every giver is filled with just one thing: love.

In his book, *The 10 Commandments of Business And How To Break Them,* Bill Fromm, the president of Barkley & Evergreen Advertising and a senior vice president of Young Presidents' Organization writes: "—The people I work with—want responsibility, recognition, education, opportunity and *love*. My job is to see they get it." (Italics added.)

Mr. Fromm is an exception, not in his application of love in his business, but in his open use of the word. My experience is that love is rarely mentioned as the underlying driving force for success, yet at the core of every successful person is the engine of love roaring away to provide the power in their being.

Love is the immortal flow of energy that nour-
ishes, extends and preserves. Its eternal goal
is life.
> —Smiley Blanton

The truth of the matter is that whether we use the word or not, love is all around us. Love is the hook word or main ingredient in more songs than any other word. Love is the centerpiece of the vast majority of all poetry. Love is the primary plot or subplot of every single motion picture that has been a whopping success. Love is the universal theme of nearly all of our great works in literature. And it is love that has inspired so many of our great masterpieces in the arts. But love is not just evident in the arts. Would we have Disney World if it were not for Walt Disney's love for children? Would we have all of our great advances in medicine if it weren't for the love of our scientists for their fellowman? Would we have more than 10,000 charities in our country if it wasn't for the power of love? I don't think so.

You are a Child of God. You were created in
a blinding flash of creativity, a primal
thought when God extended Himself in love.
> —Marianne Williamson

We were created in love and born with a seed at the core of our souls and that seed is our desire for love. All that we have become, or will become, grows from this single seed. Our desire for love contains the most awesome but perhaps the least understood of the many miracle powers we possess, yet it is surely the most basic and the most powerful of them all. In her work, *Feel the Fear and Do It Anyway,* Susan Jeffries points out the power of love and she recommends repeating these words: *I am powerful, and I am loving.* Nelson Rockefeller, governor of New York, said to Henry Kissinger, secretary of state, *Never forget that the most powerful force on Earth is love.* The seed of our desire for love is not just our personal wanting of love, however; it also is our fundamental need to *give our love to others.*

The desire and ability to give of our love is unlike any other tangible or intangible force we know. The more we love, the greater our capacity and power to love, and the greater still the joy we will receive from loving.

We all have a wanting to be loved, but more important than that is our absolute necessity to *give* our love away in whatever way is right for each of us. What each of us does with our love may be the most important choice we each have to make.

When you really think about it, love is the most self-indulgent, self-centered act there is. We may all hide behind the altruistic facade that giving of ourselves is something we do for our fellowman, but those who give know this is all a whopper of a tale—

for giving of your love is the surest and most immediate path to self-satisfaction.

If you want to instantly feel good, be happy, and
get a real high, go hug someone, flash them a smile,
lend them a hand, or send them a prayer. Just do
something nice for someone, it doesn't matter what
it is, or who you do it for. They'll be elated and you
will have thrown another coin into your own chest of
riches and rewards.

In all the universe only love violates the otherwise certainty of the law of cause and effect that what
you get is in proportion to what you give. For when
you give your love, you do not get back in proportion
to what you give, you get back manyfold. This is
always the case. You always get back more than you
give. Always.

> *If I choose to bless another person, I will
> always end up feeling more blessed.*
> —Marianne Williamson

A technique recommended by Dr. Norman
Vincent Peale in his book *The Power Of Positive
Thinking* is firing silent prayers at people.

I thought this was silly when I first read it years
ago, but I gave it a try in a business meeting the next
day. A man I was working for was being quite difficult, so I fired three silent prayers like bullets to his

forehead, simple ones, like "God bless you and your family."

Well, let me tell you, the results about knocked me out of my chair. Immediately after my third bullet-prayer, my boss literally stopped in the middle of a sentence (in which he was more or less chewing me out), smiled, and said something like, "Are you hungry? I am. Let me buy you lunch."

I have used the prayer-firing technique hundreds of times since then (probably even thousands of times) and I promise you it works. Most times when I give speeches I will fire little tiny prayers at people when our eyes meet and the immediate physical results I see in their eyes and in their expressions are amazing. If you think about it, firing a prayer has to work—it's impossible to hold anything but a pleasant disposition for someone you are consciously praying for. And when you pray for someone, you are loving them, and when you love someone, even a little bit, even for just a moment, they know.

> *Once you have learned to love, you will have*
> *learned to live.*
> — Unknown

In *How To Win Friends and Influence People,* Dale Carnegie wrote about Howard Thurston, the "Great Thurston," the extremely successful magician in the early 1900s. Carnegie explained that Thurston attributed his success to his *love* for his audience. Thurston said he never stepped in front of the footlights without first saying to himself over and over: *I love my audience. I love my audience.*

It is odd that there are only a few people like Thurston who can, and will, talk openly about their love for people, when loving others is the most natural thing we can possibly do.

> *We all need each other.*
>
> —Leo F. Buscaglia

In his book, *The 7 Habits of Highly Effective People,* Stephen Covey explains the maturation process as growing from *dependent to independent* and finally to *interdependence.* Interdependence is the ultimate stage we should be striving for in life because it is at this stage that our ultimate power, love, is at peak performance.

We are born *dependent* upon our mothers and fathers; then, in our youth, we struggle to prove our *independence.* As we mature, we begin to understand that our independence must grow into *interdependence* if we ever want to release our full powers and realize our potential. We are at full throttle only when we are interdependent—when we find people who need us as much as we need them. That is, we are at full throttle when we find someone who needs *our love* as much as we need to give it to them. This occurs, essentially, when we have found our purpose and meaning in life.

> *The only true happiness comes from squandering ourselves for a purpose.*
> —John Mason Brown

To accomplish all that you want in life, do not try to achieve your goals for yourself, for self-satisfaction will summon only the weaker of your powers; choose instead to dedicate your accomplishments to others, for that is when you will see your full power. As William James, the noted philosopher said: *The deepest principle in human nature is the craving to be appreciated.* We can achieve such a sense of appreciation only by doing for others. We can only get by giving.

Theresa Andrews, an Olympic gold medalist, swam to win for her paralyzed brother and when she did, she broke records. Said Theresa, "My coach told me that when I swim for myself, I always finish last, but when I swim for someone else, or the team, I always win." And she did.

Leo Tolstoy, the Russian writer, said: *The sole meaning of life is to serve humanity.* And in different words, this is what the Peace Corps said in its advertisements when it was founded: *Feel better about yourself than you ever thought possible.*

One of the greatest gifts in life is finding someone

who needs us, and who needs our love (and the manifestation of our love through our deeds) as much as we need to give our gifts to them. This "someone" can be a paralyzed brother as it is for Theresa Andrews, it can be the masses of the poor as they are for Mother Teresa, it can be the children in a class for a teacher, it can be a struggling child for his mother or father, it can be the people who need our Peace Corps volunteers, it can be the recipients of benefit concerts for victims of AIDS, or it can be people who need modern advances in medicine as it was for Jack Whitehead. It really doesn't matter who "it" is. It can be one person or millions.

Dr. Albert Schweitzer, the famous physician and philosopher who spent so much of his life tending to those who needed his care in Africa, put it this way: *I don't know what your destiny will be, but one thing I know: the only ones among you who will be really happy are those who will have sought and found how to serve.*

When we find "that someone" and see that they need our love and are responding to our love, then we are interdependent with them, and that provides the fuel of desire and the power to move the greatest mountains.

*When we die and go to Heaven, our Maker is
not going to say, why didn't you discover the
cure for such and such? The only thing we're
going to be asked at that precious moment is
why didn't you become you?*

—Wiesel

Don't be concerned if you don't immediately
bring to mind some big, important sounding interdependent relationship that gives meaning and purpose to your life. The realization of these relationships comes at varying times in our lives, at varying
ages. Yours will come to you, if you seek it out—if you
choose to go find it, and if you dream.

That you must do, however. You must seek out
"someone" who needs you, and then you must give
them your love the best way you know how. But don't
wait for a revelation to come your way and reveal the
meaning and purpose in your life, instead, live each
day with love and give a little of yourself to others
each day. Even a smile to lift a friend is a gift you can
give.

*He that bringeth a present findeth the door
open.*

—Thomas Fuller

I have a college professor friend who has found
that his students need him as much as he needs them.
One would have to be blind and deaf not to see the

love in my friend's classroom. There is a lot of intellectual learning going on in his classes, but that's a side benefit—the big benefits are the learning about life and the encouragement that my friend provides his students.

I know a man named Josh (fictitious name, real person) who is very, very successful in business, and I believe it is largely because Josh is extremely generous and because he always seems to be doing something nice for people. I've joked that it would be my luck that when I'm in line at the Pearly Gates I would find Josh ahead of me and Mother Teresa ahead of Josh and I would hear the Angel at the gate ask of each of them: "Couldn't you have done more?"

As Isaac Tigrett, the founder of The Hard Rock Cafe, says in his motto: *Love all; serve all.*

We can all do more, but only if we commit to our goals on behalf of others. Do this and release your ultimate secret power, your love. Do this and watch your basket of success fill itself over and over again.

If you have a choice—and must make it—between love and profit, between love and personal gain, between love and anything else on Earth, choose love. And don't be afraid to use the word.

Love.

In Sum . . .

♦ You possess the most extraordinary power in the universe—it is your love.

♦ The core of your power is not your wanting of love, nor your receipt of love, but your absolute and overriding need to give of your love to others.

♦ You will accomplish all that you want in life when you give of yourself to others.

———————

Love is all you need.
   —John Lennon and Paul McCartney

Your Ultimate Power

What To Do . . .

1. Search for individuals who need the love you have to offer as much as you need to give them your love—then give them your love the best way you know how.

2. Strive for all of your goals with a beneficiary in mind other than yourself.

3. Try the technique of firing silent little prayers at individuals. It works wonders.

4. Do something nice for someone each and every day. This can be as small as a special compliment or note of thanks or as large as you might imagine, but let not a day pass without giving of yourself to others.

What force is more
potent than love?
—Igor Stravinsky

Ten

Dare to dream, for you can have all your dreams come true.

The Sky Is Always Blue

ONE DAY years ago, I had to fly to a business meeting on a cold, cloudy, miserable day. Instead of using a covered jetway, we dashed across the tarmac in the rain to the plane. No one spoke as the plane began climbing into the storm clouds and we became engulfed in total darkness. It was eerie, and to be honest, hair-raising, since the plane was banging around like a ping pong ball in a bingo number shaker. Then it happened. We broke through the clouds and I thought we had entered Heaven itself.

Several passengers gasped, then there was silence—as though even the plane itself had become hushed. We were engulfed in nothing but blue, blue, blue.

Up until our moment of breaking through the clouds, I think most of us had forgotten that the sky *is* always blue. But once we broke through, it was impossible not to remember. As far as anyone could see—and believe me, *everyone* was looking out the windows—there was nothing but this incredible blue sky around us. We took it in for several moments, then someone broke our reverie: "Oh look!" We all turned and in the distance, there it was, a rainbow shining through a gaping hole in the clouds.

What a perspective that was! What a perspective it could be for us always. If only we would remember that above the clouds, above our rainy days, the sky *is indeed* always blue. There are going to be days when there seems to be no end to the storms raging in our lives, but don't ever forget—hang on for the blue, know that there's blue sky, sunshine, and a rainbow still out there somewhere just waiting to pop through the clouds.

When we were young, we each lived in the center of a wonderful place. Everywhere we looked, for as far as the mind's eye could see, adventure and opportunity beckoned us. In one direction, we saw majestic mountains, and we dreamed of climbing them. In another direction, we saw open seas, and we imagined sailing in great ships amidst the waves. Topping the mountains and the seas, we saw white clouds floating in blue skies, and we imagined soaring with the eagles. We were *children* and we lived in our dreams—dreams full of life.

As Mencius, the grandson of Confucius, said: *The great man is he who does not lose his child's heart.* Unfortunately, that is exactly what often happens as we make our way in the world—we begin to lose heart. Sooner or later, we begin to encounter little disappointments and find that we don't always get what we want. Maybe we encounter a lot of little disappointments and maybe even a few big ones. We start to adjust our view of the world, and the door is opened for a tragedy to occur as we grow older. We start to allow others to become our Dream Snatchers, and we permit the Anacondas of Doubt, Despair and Limitations to enter our lives, where they construct fences of confinement around us. In time, we may even pitch in and help construct those fences ourselves. Before you know it, all of our dreams have been stolen away and the fences of doubt and impossibility have become so high that the mountains and the seas are no longer in view—and the sky is no longer blue.

Eventually, we come to accept our fenced-in world as the world we must live in, and we go on living in it in fear—not in fear of death, but in fear of life.

The tragedy is that nothing has changed—

beyond our fences are the mountains and the seas yet awaiting us. The sky is still blue.

> *. . . when you look for the miracle you've got to scatter your blood to the eight points of the wind because the miracle is nowhere but circulating in the veins of man.*
> —George Seferis

All we need is to remember the miracle that we each are and recall the miraculous powers that we each have. We each have the ability to break through the clouds. We each have secret powers we have not even begun to use. What we must do is take charge of ourselves, get up off our duffs, rip down those walls, and go for the gold at the end of the rainbow. In the words of Orison Swett Marden: *The greatest trouble with most of us is that our demands upon ourselves are so feeble, the call upon the great within us so weak and intermittent that it makes no impression upon the creative energies; it lacks the force that transmutes desires into realities.*

> *Most people never run far enough on their first wind to find out if they've got a second. Give your dreams all you've got and you'll be amazed at the energy that comes out of you.*
> —William James

When we dream, we can demand of ourselves and

then go for our dreams. Growing up doesn't mean we cast aside our childhood! Growing up means being able to pursue those dreams and make them ever bigger and ever better. Dreams aren't like clothing that we grow out of. You weren't born to shed your dreams like a lowly snake sheds its skin. You were *not* born to grow out of your dreams—you were born to grow into them.

> *Youth is not a time of life, it is a state of mind. You are as old as your doubt, your fear, your despair. The way to keep young is to keep your faith young. Keep your self confidence young. Keep your hope young.*
> —Luella F. Phean

Your dreams can be hidden behind the clouds and forgotten, but they can never be lost. To find and live your dreams again, draw upon the great power of your imagination and summon the genie within you. Call upon the other powers at your fingertips, especially the power of your love. Your love can move the mountains, your love can push you through the clouds into the blue sky above.

There is a music that each of us sings as we make our choices and spend our lives, and when we stretch through the clouds toward greatness on behalf of others, that music erupts as a symphony unto the heavens.

263

As Frank Scully says: "Why not go out on a limb? Isn't that where the fruit is?" You are standing at the shoreline of life and beyond is the horizon. Your purpose in life will not come to you, nor will your dreams. You must swim out to meet them where the horizon meets the blue sky.

As Og Mandino wrote: *There is nothing as sad as the man who spends his life waiting for his ship to come in, when he never sent one out.*

The water's fine. Jump on in, and don't look back, except to lead those who follow or to lend a hand to those who need your help. Dare to soar.

God bless you.

In Sum . . .

◆ Pursue your dreams and you can have them. You are the miracle, you have the power, you really do.

◆ Remember, the sky is *always* blue.

Come to the edge, He said.
They said, We are afraid.
Come to the edge, He said.
They came.
He pushed them . . . and they flew.
　　　　　　　　　—Guillaume Apollinaire

Far away there in the sunshine are my highest aspirations. I may not reach them, but I can look up and see their beauty, believe in them, and try to follow where they lead.

—Louisa May Alcott

Acknowledgements
And
Recommended Reading

My deepest thanks and appreciation to the authors and other individuals and firms below for their wonderful works which have provided enormous contributions and guidance to my personal knowledge and development. I highly recommend each of these works:

Allen, Charles L.	◆ *All Things Are Possible Through Prayer*
Autry, James A.	◆ *Love & Profit*
Bach, Richard	◆ *Jonathan Livingston Seagull*
Bartlett, John	◆ *Bartlett's Familiar Quotations*
Bristol, Claude M.	◆ *The Magic of Believing*
Buckingham, Jaime	◆ *Power for Living*
Buscaglia, Leo F.	◆ *Born to Love* ◆ *Love*
Byrne, John	◆ *1,911 Best Things Anybody Ever Said*

Carnegie, Dale ◆ *How to Win Friends & Influence People*

Chopra, Deepak ◆ *Magic Mind, Magic Body**

Covey Stephen R. ◆ *The 7 Habits of Highly Effective People*

Cypert, Samuel A. ◆ *Believe and Achieve— W. Clement Stone's 17 Principles of Success*

Drucker, Peter F. ◆ *Managing for Results*
◆ *The Effective Executive*

Davis, Wynn ◆ *Best of Success*

Fadiman, Clifton, General Editor ◆ *The Little Brown Book of Anecdotes*

Forbes Publishing ◆ *The Forbes Scrapbook of Thoughts on the Business of Life*

Fromm, Bill ◆ *10 Commandments of Business and How to Break Them*

Gilbert, Ron ◆ *WIN!* (quotation cards)

Grey, Marilyn (with Betty Bender) ◆ *It's All in Your Head*

Haroldsen, Mark O. ◆ *The Courage to Be Rich*

Helmstetter, Shad ◆ *Choices*
◆ *What You Say When You Talk to Yourself*

Hill, Napoleon ◆ *Think & Grow Rich*

Hubbard, Elbert G.   ◆ *A Message to Garcia*
(magazine article in the
Philistine in 1899)

Mandino, Og   ◆ *A Better Way to Live*
◆ *The Choice*
◆ *The Greatest Miracle
in the World*
◆ *The Greatest Salesman
in the World*
◆ *The Return of the
Ragpicker*
◆ *Treasury of Success
Unlimited*
◆ *University of Success*

Mille, Richard de   ◆ *Put Your Mother on
the Ceiling*

Murphy, Joseph   ◆ *The Power of Your
Subconscious Mind*

Parker, Jonathan   ◆ *Build a Winning
Self Image**
◆ *The Prosperity Solution**

Peale, Norman Vincent   ◆ *Positive Imaging*
◆ *Power of the Plus Factor*
◆ *The Power of Positive
Thinking*

Schuller, Robert H.   ◆ *Possibility Thinking**

Schwartz, David J.   ◆ *The Magic of Thinking Big*

Stone, W. Clement
(with Napoleon Hill)   ◆ *Success Through Positive
Mental Attitude*

Tice, Lou	◆ *Power of Belief—* a Nightingale-Conant Insight Series presentation relating the Cliff Young story
Vance, Mike	◆ *Creative Thinking** ◆ *A Kitchen for the Mind**
Waitley, Denis	◆ *10 Seeds of Greatness* ◆ *The Psychology of Winning**
Williamson, Marianne	◆ *A Return to Love*
Ziglar, Zig	◆ *Top Performance*

* Audio tape recordings

In addition to those above, I want to thank Lewis Timberlake of Austin, Texas who taught me about epitaph planning and who provided the inspiration for me to become what I am becoming.

Thank you all.

Postscript

You may be interested in knowing that we are creating a line of posters, note cards and other similar items to serve as reminders of the principles contained in *Soar . . . If You Dare*. If you would like to receive more information about these items and be added to our mailing list, please drop us a note at the address below.

Humdinger™ Books
P.O. Box 3736
Reston, VA 22090-1736

The first miracle you need to believe in is YOU.

Whatever
understanding
you have of yourself,
that is what
you become.
You can become anything,
because the world exists
through the
power of feelings.
There is nothing fixed
about a human being.
He is whatever feeling
he has about himself.
He is what he thinks.

—Swami Muktananda, Siddha master